THE BULL HUNTER

THE
BULL HUNTER

Tracking Today's Hottest Investments

DAN DENNING

WILEY

John Wiley & Sons, Inc.

Published by John Wiley & Sons, Inc., Hoboken, New Jersey
Published simultaneously in Canada

For general information about our other products and services, please contact our Customer Care Department within the United States at 800-762-2974, outside the United States at 317-572-3993 or fax 317-572-4002.

Wiley also publishes its books in a variety of electronic formats. Some content that appears in print may not be available in electronic books. For more information about Wiley products, visit our web site at www.wiley.com.

Library of Congress Cataloging-in-Publication Data:

Denning, Dan.
  The bull hunter : tracking today's hottest investments / Dan Denning.
    p. cm.
  ISBN-13 978-0-471-71983-0 (cloth)
  ISBN-10 0-471-71983-8 (cloth)
    1. Capital investments.   2. Bull markets.   I. Title.
  HG4028.C4D45 2005
  332'.0415—dc22   2005003086

Printed in the United States of America

10   9   8   7   6   5   4   3   2   1

CONTENTS

Contents

FOREWORD

The world is in the process of shifting from one in which the United States is the primary engine of international growth to one in which there are multiple engines. This process will not be comfortable for investors and retirees who expect the investment prospects of tomorrow to be like the opportunities of the past decades.

The United States is in the midst of a long-term secular bear cycle. Given the high valuations of the broad stock market, stock market returns are likely to be modest at best in the next 10 years. U.S. bond investors are faced with low interest rates and the serious potential for rising rates, which is not a good environment for bonds.

But that does not mean investors need despair. As the saying goes, there is always a bull market somewhere. There are opportunities awaiting the investor who is willing to do a little extra homework. In *The Bull Hunter,* we get to peek over Dan Denning's shoulder and look at his homework notes, so to speak, as he travels and searches the world looking for opportunity.

While it may not be a smooth ride, the long-term trends that are now in play are setting up opportunities every bit as big as the U.S. stock and bond market in 1982.

Less than 20 years ago, China and India were mired in socialist governments and devastating poverty. Their entrepreneurs were not welcome in the halls of government. That has now changed. The desire of billions of Chinese and Indians to achieve middle-class status is one of the most compelling stories in recent history and will be one of the greatest potential builders of wealth of the new millennium. As an example, we are told that only two decades ago there were less than 60 cars in private hands in all of China. Now they produce that many every four minutes.

They will need commodities like iron, cement, nickel, aluminum, and copper, to list a few among a host of metals required as they build out their cities and homes. Where will an energy-hungry world find the power to enable such a fierce drive to improve their lot in life? Just the need for energy and raw materials to supply them is enough to create whole new bull markets.

And when you add together the populations of the nations surrounding China and India, you find another billion people with the same goals of improving not only their own lives but those of their children!

But the story is not just one of an improving environment for commodities and energy. There are far more bull markets that will be born in the coming years both at home and abroad, as entrepreneurs throughout the world will find new products and ways to serve their customers.

There are intriguing new investment vehicles like the exchange-traded funds (ETFs) and other new funds, which Dan talks about, that allow us to invest locally and safely while giving us an opportunity to be part of the global growth story.

These new bull markets are an opportunity for us to participate in this powerful new wave of free markets and capitalism. In a world where information is at our fingertips, we should not limit ourselves to yesterday's markets and our own backyard. There is now an entire world we can search for value, seeking out opportunities to improve our own portfolios and net worth. *The Bull Hunter* is a good start.

So good luck and good hunting!

John Mauldin

ACKNOWLEDGMENTS

In his 1947 essay, "Why I Write," George Orwell said: "It is bound to be a failure, every book is a failure, but I know with some clarity what kind of book I wrote." If I've achieved any clarity in this book, I had some help from some very talented and generous people.

First I'd like to thank Bill Bonner for encouraging me to write a book in the first place. Thanks to all the people at Agora who have been an influence on my thinking and investing over the years, including Steve Sjuggerud, Porter Stansberry, Dan Ferris, Alex Green, Chris Dehaemer, Karim Rahemtulla, James Boric, and especially Eric Fry. Another hearty thanks to talented investors and writers John Mauldin, Greg Weldon, Steve Belmont, Michael Checkan, and Bob Meier, Byron King, and Chet Richards.

Thanks, too, to the many people who made my trip to Asia possible and worthwhile, including Jason Kelly in Japan, Pinank Mehta in India, and Kevin Francis in Sydney. Special thanks go to Debra and Mike Yantis in Koh Samui, Thailand, and Dr. Andre Homberg and Verena Homberg in Perth, Australia, all four of whom went out of their way to introduce me to other investors and show me sights I might otherwise have missed.

Acknowledgments

And thanks to the many people who put up with my frequent e-mails, phone calls, and interminable conversations and who helped make this book possible, including Sala Kannan, who set up many of my meetings in India; Greg Grillot, Joe Schriefer, Cheryl Greene, Tom Dyson, Bob Compton, Sandy Franks, Laura Davis, and Michelle Nickels in Baltimore; and Adrian Ashe, Frank Hemsley, Brian Myers, Merryn Somerset Webb, Mike Graham, Nic Laight, and Lord William Rees-Mogg in London.

Thanks to Addison Wiggin, Thom Hickling, Jack Forde, Mike Palmer, and Jack Howley for being good critics and better friends, and to Mike Ward, Wayne Ellis, Michael C. Thomsett, Mark Ford, and Deb England for all their hard work. Thanks to my sister Virginia for making sure I got all my frequent-flyer miles, and thanks to my entire family for their loving support, of both my failures and my occasional successes.

Dan Denning
London, England
2005

THE BULL HUNTER

LIONS, EAGLES, DRAGONS, AND BULL HUNTERS: A VISION TO PROFIT

Capital investment is heavily concentrated in the goods-producing sector. Ruin that sector, and you will infallibly see less and less capital investment in the economy.

—**Dr. Kurt Richebächer**[1]

Trade, of course, predates manufacturing and has always dominated it. But it's pretty pointless if we don't make anything to trade.

—**James Dyson**[2]

It does not do to leave a live dragon out of your calculations, if you live near him.

—**J.R.R. Tolkien**[3]

Never turn down help, even if it comes from unexpected places in unexpected forms. I learned this two years ago, when I locked myself out of my apartment in Paris on July 14, Bastille Day, wearing nothing but a pair of boxer shorts and a T-shirt.

This was the summer of record heat in France. And so luckily, nobody was wearing much, even by French standards. I didn't look out of place wearing a green sarong and a pair of white terry cloth bath slippers I borrowed from a petite femme in the apartment below. I legged my way, with an occasional catcall, through the red-light district on Rue St. Denis to my office, sent an e-mail to the landlord, and waited for three hours to get a spare key. I did not keep the sarong.

Even when it's unlooked for, good fortune may be staring you in the face. So when I again locked myself out of my apartment (this time in London, after midnight, on a cold and rainy Wednesday), I was only a little surprised to get lucky again. I found a small hotel room in a place called the County Hall, just beneath the great London Eye. I turned on the TV and came face-to-face with James Dyson.

Dyson is a British vacuum cleaner magnate. He makes things for a living, instead of buying them. It's a habit that's gone out of style in America, where consuming more than you produce is now the norm.

You may recognize Dyson from TV commercials in which he hawks his products. But on this night, he was hawking something entirely different. It was a very specific idea about why the Industrial Revolution happened in England, and how England went on to become the richest, most powerful nation on earth.

Dyson showed that England got rich through what an economist would call capital-intensive investment. You and I would simply call it manufacturing. It's what made England rich. It's what's making China rich today. And Dyson claims it's how the West—or at least some investors—can get rich again. He also claims that

- "Of the world's 10 largest corporations by revenue, nine make big, heavy things. Like cars or ships' turbines or computer hardware or consumer electronics."
- "These companies rely on their engineering and their technology —not their styling—for their wealth. Only one—Wal-Mart— is a service company."
- "Look at the most profitable companies, and again, the facts speak for themselves. In the top 10, only three are service companies."

- "Only one in seven British jobs is in manufacturing, yet they generate nearly two-thirds of exports. Manufacturing creates the wealth and spending power that feed the service industry."[4]

"It's obvious," Dyson concludes, *"the rest of the world relies on manufacturing for its wealth. Why do we think we can be different? If we want to maintain our position alongside other leading nations, we've got to join the rest."* He finished with a history lesson worth keeping in mind:

History repeatedly shows the correlation between a nation's wealth and its diplomatic and military powers. Before the Industrial Revolution, Britain accounted for just one-fiftieth of the world's manufacturing output, while China spoke for a third. Fewer than a hundred years later, China had been invaded by a small British army. Its industry was now backward. Britain, with 2% of the world's population, was making nearly half the world's goods. And politically, we led the world. So if we want to protect our quality of life and our influence, we must maintain our average wealth—our GDP per capita. The only sure way to do that is to continue to innovate and manufacture. I believe manufacturing is the future, not the past.[5]

FROM ENGLISH TEXTILES TO GLOBAL FORTUNES

Dyson is not the first Englishman to rediscover what made his country great and what is currently enabling China to clobber the rest of the West economically. Knowing I was interested in the history of how the West got rich, a colleague asked me to review a book called *Capital and Innovation,* by Charles Foster (Arley Hall Press, 2004).

The book reached many of the same conclusions as Dyson did about what made England rich. Foster's book is about the economic development of Cheshire and Lancashire counties from 1500 to 1780, which led to the Industrial Revolution in England. It is really a case study of the world's first industrial economy and its foremost maritime, trade, and military power. *England leapt ahead of the rest of the world and stayed there for nearly 300 years because Englishmen began saving, investing, and trading.* They saved money from lands that became profitable farms. They invested in new technologies to make the lands more productive (the steam engine, for example). And they traded their newly manufactured goods with their American cousins.

It's really a simple story of individual actions making a nation rich. A good example is Peter Warburton. In 1575 he inherited his father's estate. The total value of his father's possessions at his death was £773. Peter began purchasing leases to increase his income, rather than only farming the land. By the time he died 51 years later, his inherited possessions were worth £12,613—a 1,500 percent increase.

What's even more important is that more than £9,000 of his personal worth was in gold and silver coins. His leases and tithes brought in £1,146 in income. His cattle stock had grown to 213 head, only four more than his father's 209. But because of rising land and grain values, the cattle had doubled in value. Peter Warburton had turned a farm and his leases into a source of passive income for the accumulation of capital.

He was not alone. Dozens of tenants and families were doing the same thing all across England. These families were also developing important traditions that still serve as the bedrock of a healthy economy. They were saving. They viewed their capital as an asset for the wealth of future generations.

As they accumulated capital, all the benefits of investment began to show up in the northwest. Foster explains that employment in the region expanded. Fathers had money to send their sons to London to become doctors and lawyers. And because families were able to accumulate wealth in a liquid form (cash instead of land), more children inherited money than under the previous regime. This had the effect of capitalizing even more future entrepreneurs.

CAN IT WORK TODAY?

Can this sixteenth-century model of economic success really work today? I'll argue later that it already is working—in China. It is now broken in the United States of America.

Companies like General Motors and Ford—which used to be manufacturing giants—have transformed themselves into hedge funds, making more money on their financing operations than on the manufacture and sale of cars. As a whole, the American economy doesn't invest enough money in building things. Today's America (as I'll show later) invests in less durable types of assets. The respected economist, Dr. Kurt Richebächer, explains. The Austrian school of economics shows that savings and investment, not credit and consumption, are the foundation of growing economies. Dr. Richebächer writes of the overall decline in American investment spending and notes:

> No less ominous is the shift in the composition of investment spending between different sectors of the economy. Overall investment in information processing is up 20% since 2000, computers making up 84.3% of that. But investment in industrial equipment is down 12.4%, and transportation investment down even 19.2%. It seems a reasonable assumption that the investment spending on information high-tech is centered in the economy's growth sectors, such as retail trade and finance. Investment in industrial equipment is no higher today than in 1995.
>
> Manifestly, manufacturing is the key trouble spot in the U.S. economy. With a loss of almost 3 million jobs, from 17 million, since 2000, the sector accounts singularly for the overall job disaster. All other major sectors had rising employment. Not surprisingly, manufacturing stands out with the weakest investment spending.[6]

This ailment is not a run-of-the-mill cold. It's chronic. And it has real long-term consequences. The doctor continues:

> It should immediately be clear that this extraordinary investment weakness is structural, not cyclical, and just as clear also should be its main cause: grossly overexpanded consumer spending, essentially at the expense of saving, investment, production, and the trade balance.
>
> Changes in business capital investment play a crucial role in the process of economic growth through their specific effects on employment, incomes, and profits. There appears to be a widespread view that higher investment essentially reduces consumption. The fact is, rather,

7

that—through the rising production of capital goods—it increases employment and labor income more rapidly than the outflow of capital goods.

We hasten to add that this was true throughout the more than 100 years of Industrial Revolution. This technology involved huge investments in plant and equipment, of which a large part required prolonged production processes. Companies needed numerous workers to meet the huge demand for those capital goods; and once these were manufactured and installed, other firms hired workers to operate them. This investment-driven economic growth was inherently associated with strong growth of employment and incomes.

Lack of capital investment is America's present key problem. That is one reason. The second one is that the new high-tech, for which corporate managers in America have an absolute preference, has very low labor and capital intensity. Between 2000 and 2003, employment by the manufacturers of computers and electronic products plunged from 1.8 million to 1.3 million.[7]

TOMORROW'S ECONOMY OR YESTERDAY'S MISTAKE?

Even on an empty stomach, Dyson's speech was a revelation. When you add in the thoughts of Charles Foster and Dr. Kurt Richebächer, you begin to get a clearer picture of what leads to economic prosperity. But it's virtually unrecognizable today.

What you hear these days is that we're in a "postindustrial" economy. In this fictional economy, personal wealth is generated through rising asset prices and credit-financed consumption. We feel rich buying things instead of getting rich making them.

Now, I've traveled to quite a few places across the world in the last five years including China, India, Japan, Thailand, France, Germany, Italy, England, Mexico, Canada, Australia, and, of course, America. I can assure you that in nearly all of these places, spending money is not a good way to get rich.

What I've seen in all of these places—and from working in the stock market day after day for the last seven years—is a different picture of how to get wealthy that's emerging. I'll tell you some of what

I've seen and discovered in the following pages. I'll also tell you about some of the risks you face if you live, work, and invest in America.

But the most important thing I can tell you is that all over the world, fortunes are being made in more ways than you or I can imagine. For investors, it's as if you woke up one day and found you had 10 times more investment opportunities the night before. The only catch, as you rub the sleep out of your eyes, is figuring out how to profit.

BULL MARKETS ARE DEAD! LONG LIVE BULL MARKETS

For the past 20 years, most investors have viewed the stock market as a foolproof retirement machine. Find the best stocks early and hold them for a long time and you'll retire *really* rich.

But over the last four years, it's become clear that you can't automatically get wealthy buying stocks . . . if stocks aren't in a perpetual bull market. The retirement machine is sputtering. Maybe it's even broken. What do you do?

I have good news for you. The old way of making money in the stock market doesn't work anymore and it's been replaced by something better. Instead of achieving your goals by "being bullish,"—a strategy that won't work if stocks go sideways for 20 years—you redefine *bull market*.

WHAT'S A BULL AND WHAT'S A BEAR

The traditional definitions of bull and bear signify the direction of market prices. If the Dow goes up, it's bullish and we're in a bull market. If it goes down, it's bearish and we're in a bear market.

This leads to the common, but now faulty, belief that the best way to make money investing is to buy stocks only when they are going up. You *can* make money when stocks go down. Bears do it all the time. But it's considered riskier and, by some bulls, in poor taste to profit from falling prices. It's better to be a small boat, lifted by a rising tide. Right?

Every morning I cross the Thames river by walking south across the Waterloo Bridge to the south bank. The Thames is an estuarial river, which means it's close to the sea and its current is affected by the tides. Some mornings the tide is going out and the river is low. Sometimes the tide is coming in (if I'm late to work) and the river literally flows upstream. Either way, the tide is always coming or going, and the flow of the river is always changing.

The tide is coming and going in the world's investment markets, too—everywhere and all the time. Money moves quickly these days. Global capital flows faster than any river. Capital movements cause prices for stocks, bonds, or commodities to rise rapidly in one place, or fall just as rapidly in another.

For investors, the problem is that the tides of global finance are not as predictable as the tides of the Thames. If every market is a river, there are thousands of rivers. You can make money in any single one of them, and you can do so in any number of ways (as I'll show you later).

The key thing is to realize that you have many choices. The terms *bull* and *bear* are simply not relevant today. Beyond the Dow Jones Industrials, mutual funds, and Vanguard index funds is a whole universe of investment opportunities. Today, you can buy Chinese ball-bearing makers, invest in the best companies in Australia, profit from a booming demand in cemented carbide metal-cutting tools, or even trade options and futures—all from your own home.

Sometimes you'll profit when prices rise, sometimes when they fall. It may be a stock, a bond, a currency, or a commodity. But as you cast your investment glance across the globe, you'll see the world has changed to your advantage. In this book, I'll show you precisely what I've seen and how I think you can turn this change into investment profits. Of course, not everyone is comfortable with the idea that the investment rules have changed. It means changing your perspective. But it takes only a slight change to see what I'm talking about.

For example, it's a common but mistaken belief that the investment terms *bull* and *bear* come from the way that these animals approach their respective foes. A bear moves his paw in a downward motion and a bull thrusts his horns upward. In fact, back in the days when traders hunted animals, so-called bear skin jobbers were fur traders who sold skins from bears they had not yet caught. Think of this as an early futures contract. You got a fixed price today for a commodity to be delivered at a later date. By doing this you hedge your risk that the future price might be less than today's price. But you also risk getting less for your commodity than it will be worth.

For this reason, the term came to describe anyone who sold short on any stock share or commodity. The use of *bull* as the opposite derives from the old practice of pitting bears and bulls against each other as a form of sport. Incidentally, Paris Garden in Southwark is one of the old places where bull and bear baitings were staged in sixteenth- and seventeenth-century London. It's only five minutes' walk from the office I work at today.

LONDON AND MODERN FINANCE

It's no accident that essential terms like *bull* and *bear* come from capitalism's early growth in London. The English got rich by thinking about making money in new ways. It's a skill that Americans picked up, too. It's also absolutely essential if you want to profit in an increasingly complex and interconnected global economy.

As long ago as 1785, today's version of *bull* and *bear* were defined by Thomas Mortimer in his book, *Every Man His Own Broker.* Mortimer wrote:

> [A] man who in March buys in the Alley [reference to the exchange in old London, Exchange Alley] 40,000 pounds [for settlement] in May, and at the same time is not worth ten pounds in the world . . . is a Bull, till such time as he can discharge himself of his heavy burden by selling it to another person . . ."

Even then, the English humor was understated. But Mortimer was not finished. He defines a bear as

> . . . a person who has agreed to sell any quantity of the public funds more than he is possessed of, and often without being possessed of any at all, which, nevertheless, he is obliged to deliver against a certain time: before

11

this time arrives, he is continually going up and down seeking . . . whose property he can devour; you will find him in a continual hurry; always with alarm, surprise, and eagerness painted in his countenance; greedily swallowing the least report of bad news; rejoicing in mischief, or any misfortune that may bring about the wished-for change of falling the stocks, that he may buy in low, and so settle his accounts to advantage.

Mortimer captured the psychology of bulls and bears perfectly. But his observations apply equally well today to traditional bull and bear investing or, more accurately, to long and short strategies. Today's bulls are generally pie-in-the-sky optimists. Today's bears are generally doom-and-gloom pessimists (although it might be more fair to call them realists).

But what if you expand on Mr. Mortimer's ancient advice? What if you combine the two traditional ways of making money in stocks with the modern world's constant shifting investment tides and capital flows? If you do, you begin to see the vast possibility for investment profits in today's world. It might look something like this:

A bull market is an opportunity to profit from the change in price of any given asset in any part of the world at any time. The opportunity might be rising stock prices or falling bond prices. It could be rising sugar prices or falling steel prices. Or it could be a booming economy in Norway and a falling euro in Europe.

The key to profitable investing in the world you're going to live in for the next 20 years is equating *bull* with the word *opportunity*. It simply doesn't matter whether the price direction is upward, downward, or sideways (yes, there is opportunity even in that).

Proper bull hunters follow their quarry wherever in the world it might be. They aren't misled by crowds or investor sentiment, nor are they bound by old rules that don't work. They recognize that in a world teeming with markets—stock markets, bond markets, commodity markets, options markets, currency markets—there is abundant opportunity, *if* they have the wits and the courage to see them.

I'm talking here about a strategic vision for investment profits in the world as it is today and tomorrow, and as it will be for the next 20 years. In this world, there's no good reason to limit yourself to the traditional ideas of buying low and selling high.

You can do better. A bull hunter acknowledges that you can also profit if you sell high and buy low (short-selling) *or* eschew buying and employ leverage (buy options instead of stocks) *or* spread risk and buy a basket of stocks instead of a single stock (avoid individual stocks and hedge your risk to a falling dollar with highly liquid pooled investments—see Chapter 3).

In other words, there are many, many different ways to invest. America itself is in the fight of its economic life. The federal government faces record yearly deficits and long-term debts. The economy faces stiff challenges from places like India and China, where labor is cheap, and Russia and Iran, where energy is abundant.

If you want to profit from these events, you first have to understand them. That takes insight, strategy, and good execution. You'll get all of that (and more, I hope) in the pages that follow.

THE END OF AMERICA?

You'll soon learn that not everything about the new competitive world is necessarily good news for America's economy. But it's essential to remember that empires and national fortunes come and go. Personal fortunes can be preserved and even grown—especially in times of great historical change.

England, for example, dominated the world for more than a century, both economically and militarily. Then came the first world war. Afterward, the world's financial system began to buckle under the stress of huge war debts. Trade fell as national rivalries grew.

Global stock markets tottered in 1929. Then came the banks. Between 1929 and 1931, the world's fragile economic system stumbled along from crisis to crisis. Everyone knew there were problems. Everyone knew how those problems had ended in the past. But the endgame always seemed to be just over the horizon.

Then, one fine day in September of 1931, it all began to go to hell, especially for England. England's currency, the pound sterling, had been the world's dominant currency. It was to that time in history what the dollar is to today's economy. Suddenly, 10 years of steady deterioration gave way to total collapse. As one commentator wrote, "Great acceleration towards the end is a common property of financial crises—most of which can seem manageable for months or years before the period of acceleration begins."[8]

America's stock market and her economy are vulnerable to a sudden and negative acceleration. Most investors won't see it coming. And most will suffer accordingly. But I will show you that even America's worst problems can be turned into opportunities with the new tools that are now available. Furthermore, there is an even wider arrange of opportunities that simply weren't available to most investors 10 years ago. I'll show you what those are, too, and how to profit from them.

FROM CRISIS TO PROFITS

Jim Rogers has traveled around the world more than any investor I know. At an investment conference at which both he and I were speaking, he made a plea to investors to consider investing outside America's borders and outside her currency, the dollar. To paraphrase what he said: If you got all of your money out of England before the pound collapsed in 1931, you would have been able to come back in later and buy up the whole country for a song.

Many people view the recent crisis in the dollar as the end of America's era of economic and financial dominance. Others say the rise of the East comes on the heels of the decline of the West, as night follows day. It wouldn't be the first time the leadership of the global economy changed hands with the end of a currency. England was a colossus of trade and power in the nineteenth century. It had the strongest currency in the world, the best navy, and the mightiest factories. It was the economic, military, and industrial power center of the world.

Yet England eventually ceded that role to America. Just as Great Britain's power and influence gave way to America, today America appears be ceding that role to China. The lion gave way to the eagle. Perhaps now the eagle is now giving way to the dragon.

But that doesn't mean you have to sit idly by and watch your economic and investment prospects get wiped out. Whether the United States rediscovers the secret to healthy, lasting economic growth, whether it frees itself from the burden of chronic deficits and devastating personal debt loads—none of that matters to bull hunters.

Bull hunters invest where there is money to be made, and it makes no difference whether it's in Topeka, Kansas, or Tokyo, Japan. In fact, if you're worried that it's not patriotic to make money while the American government goes bankrupt, I urge you to reconsider. The best thing you can do as a patriotic American today is to make your fortune wherever and however you can so that no matter what happens in Washington, you have the means to provide for your family and friends if times *do* get hard.

The nation faces formidable challenges. But the best investment response is to *not* be at the mercy of things that are out of your control. Instead, develop a strategy to regain control of your investment future.

It might help to start by looking where the biggest risks are. First you want to make sure you're aware of them. Second, you want to avoid losing money because of them. Third, you want to turn them into opportunities for profit.

REVENGE OF THE OLD ECONOMY

My investment forecast for the U.S. economy is gloomy. The major economic trends of the next few years will be rising interest rates, falling house prices, and falling bond prices. Assets that went up in price because interest rates were low and money was easy to borrow will now go down in price. And it might not be a smooth decline. You could witness a *three-sigma* event—the kind of financial implosion that professional risk managers consider highly unlikely from a statistical perspective, but that seem to happen with alarming frequency.

The near-term future bodes poorly for financial stocks. With U.S. interest rates rising, the leveraged economy will continue to unwind and the flow of easy money into paper assets will dry up. Financial assets will deflate. As an investor, it will make sense to sell "paper" and buy "stuff."

UNDERNEATH THE ECONOMY'S HOOD

When you sell paper and buy stuff, you buy assets that have enduring value and that don't fluctuate in perceived value when interest rates rise, as financial stocks, real estate investment trusts (REITs), and some mortgage lenders do.

The second reason is that certain industrial stocks are in sectors of the American economy that are *already* running a trade surplus. That's right, a surplus! You hear a lot about deficits these days. But what you may not know is that if the dollar falls even more in the near future, some American firms will become even more competitive.

For example, take a look at Tables I.1 and I.2, from a recent report about the U.S. trade deficit. Buried in the gloomy trade deficit news is evidence that certain types of investments are going to survive globalization a lot better than others. The clues are in the data. Table I.1 shows the sectors of the economy that actually increased their trade in a month when the United States ran its worst deficit in history (November 2004)! Table I.2 ranks the largest monthly percentage increases in the trade of goods during this awful period. But *both* tables support the bull hunter philosophy. Even in the midst of the

TABLE I.1 TOP 10 LARGEST NOMINAL INCREASES MONTH-OVER-MONTH

10.	Meat and poultry	+$20 million
9.	Parts, civilian aircraft	+$29 million
8.	Agri-farming unmanufactured	+$30 million
7.	Animal feeds	+$34 million
6.	Gem diamonds	+$36 million
5.	Chemicals, inorganic	+$39 million
4.	Chemicals, organic	+$56 million
3.	Petroleum products, other	+$82 million
2.	Nuclear fuel materials	+$133 million
1.	Artwork, antiques, stamps, etc.	+$147 million

Source: U.S. Department of Commerce, Bureau of Economic Analysis

**TABLE I.2   TOP 10 LARGEST PERCENTAGE INCREASES,
MONTH-OVER-MONTH**

10.	Oil seeds, food oils	+9.2%
9.	Chemicals, inorganic	+10%
8.	Maritime engines, parts	+10.6%
7.	Nonfarm tractors and parts	+14%
6.	Animal feeds	+14%
5.	Electric energy	+17%
4.	Agriculture farming, unmanufactured	+22%
3.	Art, artwork, antiques	+48%
2.	Numismatic coins	+50%
1.	Nuclear materials	+126%

Source: U.S. Department of Commerce, Bureau of Economic Analysis

worst trading performance on record, there are mini–bull markets going on right here in America. By finding out what they are, you can track down other opportunities.

As these figures show, and as you'll see later, you make money selling things you produce, not buying things other people sell. Manufacturing—and not services—has tremendous economic multiplier effects. It creates higher employment, higher incomes, more efficient use of savings, and trade surpluses. Until these statistics are understood, America's economic competitiveness will continue to go the way of the dodo. America is at risk of turning into a has-been industrial power with weakened economic and military influence across the globe.

The dollar is the most visible symbol of that decline. But it's not the only one. In Chapter 1, we'll take a look at the three biggest threats to the economy and the stock market.

O BRAVE NEW WORLD . . .

Today's bull hunter, like the fifteenth-century explorer, needs to question not only what is visible and what is believed today, but also what lies beyond the visible horizon. That's one of the reasons I've personally spent so much time on the road in the last three years. To understand the world you have to see it. I'll tell you what I've seen.

Columbus, a bull hunter of his day, was not trying to prove that the world was round—educated people of those times already knew that. His quest was economic. He realized that European power and influence were going to depend on finding a more efficient trade route. That is an obvious and simple idea, but in his times it was heard with much doubt.

Like Columbus in his time, today's bull hunter seeks a new world. We begin our journey with a critical examination of the *old* investment strategies. Chapter 1 explains why these strategies no longer work and how you begin the twenty-first century in the fight of your economic life.

DEBT, DEFICITS, AND THE DOLLAR: AMERICA'S KILLER Ds AND WHY THE OLD INVESTMENT STRATEGIES DON'T WORK

People for the most part stood their ground, but the ground itself gave way beneath them.

—**Joseph Schumpeter**[1]

Take a good look at the world around you. Oil prices are at record highs. The dollar has been globally battered. Interest rates are rising. America is clearly in the economic street fight of its life.

Why? Globalization has made the brave new investment world much more competitive. With offshoring and outsourcing showing no signs of slowing down, no job is clearly safe anymore. The automobile and aerospace industries, which America used to dominate, now face fierce competition from Japan and Europe. Even U.S. stocks and bonds and the dollar itself are not as universally popular as they were just three years ago. It's as if investors suddenly realized that there is more to the investment world than mutual funds.

But there's more than just a change in investment fashions. The old answers to basic investment questions just don't work anymore. Mutual funds are too big and slow to profit from the rapid tidal shifts in markets that are now happening. (In Chapter 2, I'll give you a specific

21

example of the rapid shifts I'm talking about, and tell you how to survive them and profit.) Most important for investors, being good at just one style of investing—value investing, growth investing, market timing—isn't enough to guarantee you'll make money in the market.

Terrorism, politics, energy prices—all of these factors affect stock values. The world is networked and complicated, and markets never sleep. Investors need new tools to keep up. The old ones clearly haven't.

But there *are* solutions, and they are both exciting and dynamic. Whether you use them depends on your willingness to take a fresh look at the investment world. And it *is* a world, not just a stock, a sector, or even an individual country. The wonder child of twentieth-century investing—the growth mutual fund—will not meet your needs in the coming years. Look at the predictions by some of the world's most respected investors. These are men who made money in the old world. They know that things are different now.

- Bill Gross, the best fixed-income manager in the country and head of the nation's largest mutual fund, the Pimco Total Return Fund, says that bonds will outperform U.S. stocks over the next decade—and that bonds will yield only low, single-digit returns.

- Warren Buffett, who turned every $10,000 he invested in Berkshire Hathaway 35 years ago into more than $18.6 million, says the Standard & Poor's 500 (S&P 500) will be lucky to eke out a 5 to 6 percent annual return over the next decade.

- Sir John Templeton, founder of Templeton Funds, recently said: "Over the next century you should expect your share prices to average 6% (return) a year. Over the next five years, ten years, I think you'll be lucky to come out even."[2]

These are gloomy forecasts for investors reluctant to use new tools. But there is no escaping reality. Mutual funds are set up to fail because of the restrictive and conservative assumptions by which managers run their funds. For the most part, fund management is out of touch with both fundamental analysis *and* market realities. Fund managers use diversification formulas that largely ignore the risks of buying into particular sectors and stocks, in the belief that their job is to spread risk and not necessarily to avoid it.

Ironically, this changes the playing field, the rules, and even the shape of the ball. If you are using a full-commission brokerage firm's advice and investing in the traditional manner of the twentieth century, you may want to lower your expectations. We face a crisis and a challenge. In fact, this challenge is the biggest that U.S. investors have had to face for the past 75 years. Traditional forms of diversification are bankrupt.

The average U.S. money market fund pays less than 3 percent. Government bond yields are coming off the lowest level in 42 years and don't promise savers much in the way of passive income that outpaces inflation. And U.S. stocks are still expensive by any fundamental measure. Then there are the intangibles: war, growing government deficits, sluggish job growth, and international outsourcing—all on top of the highest level of consumer debt and the lowest savings rates in history.

With all this going on—and the economy mired in a perpetual "recovery"—U.S. stock investments won't give you the kind of return you need to send your kids through college or finance your retirement. Yet despite this being one of the toughest investment periods in U.S. history, one fact continues to ring true to this day: *There is always a bull market going on in some corner of the world that will make investors very rich.*

Keep the positive in mind . . . because right now, we need to confront something very negative—what I call America's Killer Ds: debt, the dollar, and the deficits. You may have heard of them. If you haven't, let me introduce you to

- Chronic federal deficits ($477 billion in 2004) and a monstrous federal debt ($7 trillion)
- A $600 billion annual trade deficit
- Household debt of $9 trillion, including $2 trillion in credit card debt

- A currency, the dollar, weakened by all that debt and the enormous trade gap

The total debt picture in America is both gruesome and appalling. There is no polite way of putting it. We are a nation that cannot stop spending, even if it's money we don't have, even if it means the death of currency as a trusted source of stable value, even if it ruins our current economic prospects and dooms our children to paying off our spending sprees. See Table 1.1 for more detail on America's increasing debt.

While some of the economic relationships are complex, anyone with a sense of decency understands the problem clearly:

- You cannot spend more than you earn and get rich.
- You cannot consume more than you produce and accumulate wealth.
- You cannot borrow today and force other generations to pay without ushering in a day of reckoning.

That day is coming. The United States must import $1.8 billion in capital each day to keep the dollar from falling even more. It's been

TABLE 1.1 NATIONAL DEBT

Date	Total ($ Trillions)
1/20/2005	7.613
9/30/2004	7.379
9/30/2003	6.783
9/30/2002	6.228
9/28/2001	5.807
9/29/2000	5.674
9/30/1999	5.656
9/30/1998	5.526
9/30/1997	5.413

Source: U.S. Treasury Department Bureau of the Public Debt, www.publicdebt .treas.gov/opd/opdpdodt.htm

said that a weaker dollar, in economic theory, should make some American exporters more competitive by lowering prices for American goods overseas. But what will the Chinese buy from the United States that they can't get at a lower price from a Chinese producer? In what industry does a 30 percent decline in the dollar suddenly make American manufactured goods price-competitive with goods produced in Asia?

These are critical questions that I'll address in later chapters, where I tell you what I saw in China when I visited and what the Chinese themselves are saying. For one, I think big multinational firms may have the advantage in surviving a falling dollar. Critics of the falling dollar point out that the dollar has to fall against something, namely, another currency. That, of course, is exactly what the dollar has been doing. "But can Europe afford a stronger euro?" they ask. Maybe not. A stronger euro puts pressure on euro zone exporters.

The answer may lie in this argument: The dollar will fall against *real assets.* Chapter 2, examines what we expect to see for the dollar, the Dow, and U.S. bonds from here.

NEW REALITY, NEW STRATEGY

It is important to keep in mind that there *are* solutions. It's just that buying stocks automatically is not one of them. At times it helps to ask simple questions: What's out there that could move stock prices up this month? If I can't answer that question simply and sensibly, I usually don't buy. Are stocks cheap? Are earnings growing? Has the geopolitical situation changed in a way that moves a roadblock out of the way of higher stock prices? Or am I just hoping stocks go higher because I'm impatient?

To use the language of the Federal Reserve, I'd say the balance of risks in today's market—for U.S. stocks, that is—is negative. Stocks are still valued above historical norms. Instead of finding a reason to defend or explain this away (and buy stocks), I take it for what it's worth.

This epic bear market began in 2000. Yet the average investor has never really thrown in the towel on tech stocks. Stocks like Yahoo, Cisco, Lucent, and Microsoft are *still* the most actively traded stocks on the market. That's why you haven't yet seen the rock-bottom valuations that would trigger a buy signal. What could cause investors to pay even more for earnings than they do now? Expectations that earnings in coming fiscal quarters will be even stronger? GDP growth of 5 percent? Better growth in profits?

Maybe. But if you ask me, this is a market that's already priced as if good things were going to happen in the economy and that rising interest rates were *good* for economic growth. In other words, stocks continuously discount a positive economic scenario—well ahead of that scenario actually materializing. Yet on the other side of the ledger there are plenty of risks:

- The extra boost to consumers of tax cuts and low interest rates has run out of steam.
- Rising interest rates and oil prices will drag consumer spending down.
- Home equity withdrawals and cash-out refinancing will wane as mortgage rates rise.

These are all big risks to the American consumer. But the biggest risk of all is that America's entire economy has become more *financial* and less *tangible*. Or, if you will, more fictitious and less real. This is one of the reasons I'm so excited about opportunities elsewhere. And even here, in America's "asset economy" as Morgan Stanley analyst Steven Roach has called it, there are opportunities. But to understand the nature of the opportunities, you have to first understand the nature of the asset beast and what created it.

WHAT'S A FINANCIAL ECONOMY?

You may have heard some people claim that as an economy matures, it becomes less industrial and more service-oriented. It naturally adds more jobs in services and fewer jobs in manufacturing. This is what some people call a postindustrial economy. In the Introduction, I showed you that there's nothing wrong—and indeed a lot *right!*—about the "old" industrial economy. After all, it's how most great nations have become rich.

But what do I mean when I use the term *financial economy?* Simple, it's an economy distorted by the easy availability of credit, credit made available by the policies of a nation's central bank. Let me quote analyst Dr. Marc Faber on the subject:

> In a real economy, the debt and equity markets as a percentage of GDP are small and are principally designed to channel saving into investments. In a financial economy or "monetary driven" economy, the capital market is far larger than GDP and not only channels savings into investments but also continuously into colossal speculative bubbles. . . . In a financial economy . . . investment manias and stock market bubbles are so large that, when they burst, considerable economic damage follows.
>
> [I]n the financial economy (a disproportionately large capital market compared to the economy), the unlimited availability of credit leads to speculative bubbles, which get totally out of hand. In other words, whereas every bubble will create some "white elephant" investments (investments that don't make any economic sense under any circumstances), in financial economies' bubbles, the quantity and aggregate size of "white elephant" investments is of such a colossal magnitude that the economic benefits that arise from every investment boom . . . can be more than offset by the money and wealth destruction that arises during the bust. This is so because, in a financial economy, far too much speculative and leveraged capital becomes immobilized in totally unproductive "white elephant" investments.[3]

Those "white elephant" investments are the stocks, bonds, and mutual funds that have been bid up to incredible heights and bought with borrowed money. That *is* the financial economy. You can directly measure it in two ways: first, by how large its capital markets are relative to the total value of goods and services exchanged (GDP), and second, by the stock market capitalization–to–GDP ratio. In both cases, you're measuring *real* economic activity versus *financial,* or these days *speculative,* activity.

Let's look at the first, total credit market debt as a percentage of GDP. According to the Federal Reserve's Flow of Funds report from 2004, total credit market debt outstanding is $33.7 trillion. GDP, however, is $11.2 trillion. *In plain math, the total credit market debt outstanding is three times larger than America's GDP. Households, businesses, and government . . . everyone in America has borrowed heavily against the promise of the future.*

The biggest borrowers are financial companies. Financial debt grew by 107 percent from 1997 to 2003, doubling from $5.5 trillion to $11.4 trillion. Wall Street was busy borrowing cheap and buying expensive stocks. See Table 1.2.

It's not much better once you get off Wall Street, however. Nonfinancial debt includes the federal government, state and local governments, businesses, and households—everyone who tries to make money buying stocks (instead of selling them).

TABLE 1.2   GDP FOR COUNTRIES WITH OVER $1 TRILLION GLOBAL GROWTH RATES (AMOUNTS IN TRILLIONS OF DOLLARS)

Country	$ (in Trillions)
European Union	$11.050
United States	$10.990
China	$6.449
Japan	$3.582
India	$3.033
Germany	$2.271
United Kingdom	$1.666
France	$1.661
Italy	$1.550
Brazil	$1.375
Russia	$1.282
(total)	$44.909
Other countries	$6.561
Total world	$51.480

Source: CIA, *The World Factbook*, www.cia.gov/cia/publications/factbook

The federal government, of course, is a big offender. The federal deficit (and the national debt) are dangerous because they divert savings away from real investment. The Britons who financed the Industrial Revolution in England didn't do it by loaning money to the king. They did it by loaning money to men like Thomas Newcomen so he could make a steam engine. The steam engine became the workhorse for the Industrial Revolution, until it was replaced by the internal combustion engine.

It's not just a historical point, either. In fact, it's as important a point as realizing the breadth and depth of your investment opportunities in the gobalized world. Loaning money to the government—especially the U.S. government, which could very well default on its debt—is a fool's bargain. Chapter 2 explains how to make a much more profitable bargain from the disaster that is the U.S. government's finances.

It's a much better deal than expecting "safe" returns from U.S. savings bonds. Those bonds cannot make you rich. In fact, the more of them there are, the worse it is for America. I know this goes against conventional investment thinking. So let's take a moment to see why.

HAYEK VERSUS KEYNES: A RECAP OF BASIC ECONOMICS

John Maynard Keynes is the famous economist who advised governments to spend money in order to create economic growth. Keynes gave his now famous advice during the Great Depression, when no one—business, individuals, or the government—had money to spend. But the government enjoys the legal privilege of spending money it doesn't have. And that's what Keynes recommended. To be fair to Keynes, he didn't recommend perpetual deficit spending. His view was that government should spend only to stimulate the economy when business and the private sector are unwilling and unable. Once the government gets the economy going again, the deficit spending ought to stop. Continued deficit spending with annual increases in government spending leads to a structural deficit.

Where this version veers off into the land of economic make-believe is that a government—any government—could spend just enough money to get the economy going without succumbing to the temptation of buying votes through chronic overspending. Politicians love spending money they don't have to get votes they desperately need. They've always done so and probably always will, if we let them get away with it.

There's also a kind of intellectual sleight of hand to this thinking. The conjurer's trick is to convince you that the economy is a machine that can be operated by skilled, well-informed, monetary engineers. It's not. It's a living thing, made up of thinking people like you and me who react in a million different ways to a billion different scenarios. Markets are organic, not mechanical. Trying to treat them as machines only fouls them up.

Of course, flaws in thinking come from flaws in people. People are born flawed and die only a little improved, if they're lucky. A proper understanding of Keynes would be that it's preposterous to assume that governments, run by flawed planners with incomplete knowledge, can organize the economic lives of millions of people.

A comparison to Friedrich Hayek might help. Hayek belongs to the Austrian school of economics. To keep it simple, this school believes that markets work better than governments. Their economic theory is that wealth is created when people are allowed to make choices and take risks based on the unique information or advantage they have in the marketplace. This is the entire principle behind the bull-hunting philosophy. When people compete freely, prices are lowered and services improved. Life gets better!

More important, free of government intervention or confiscation of wealth, standards of living improve, sometimes in huge leaps and bounds. This is what Charles Foster proved about England in *Capital and Innovation* (see Introduction)—namely, that free people are innovative people, and innovative people create wealth and new opportunity. Governments do not.

Unfortunately, we live in an era of high taxes, high government spending, more government intervention in the economy, and interest rates that punish savers. If anything, the government has done more to hurt us than help us. It's destroyed the purchasing power of the currency, imposed enormous financial burdens on future unborn generations, and failed to properly secure the borders—one of the chief purposes for which this government was instituted. This amounts to nothing less than a betrayal of American ideals.

You can take back those ideals by taking responsibility for your financial future. Having the means to be self-sufficient is a huge head start in the "brave new world," where so many people depend on the government for so much. Call it a golden parachute. Call it the era of sovereign individuals, who must take care of themselves and their families because, one by one, the old institutions are failing. And call it what we're after for ourselves and our children when we decide to be bull hunters.

WHERE DID ALL THE MONEY GO?

The total federal debt, at over $4 trillion, is only 18 percent of total nonfinancial debt. This does not include future obligations to recipients of Social Security and Medicare benefits (which are rising faster than just about anything else in the economy). That number is closer to $44 trillion (yes, that's *trillion*).

American households have not exactly been paragons of responsibility. From 1997 to 2003, household debt grew from $5.5 trillion to $9.4 trillion, and continues to grow. In that time, mortgage debt grew by almost 80 percent, from $3.8 trillion in 1997 to $6.8 trillion in 2003. Consumer credit grew from $1.3 trillion to $2 trillion.

But the real growth item has been mortgage debt. And as long as we're talking about unpleasant subjects, we may as well bring up the housing bubble. I realize you might not agree with my analysis. I hope you'll consider it, though. Even if I'm wrong about my forecast, I have discovered some ways to be wrong about the big picture and still make money! I'll tell you about them in Chapter 5.

Keep in mind that I'm not against home ownership. Taking on debt to buy a house is a way to turn a liability into an asset. As long as your mortgage payment isn't a huge chunk of your monthly disposable income, and as long as you don't pay too much or buy too much house, you'll end up, eventually, with a very tangible asset: a roof over your head. But if you pay too much or borrow too much, then the asset starts to look an awful lot like a liability—or worse, a burden.

HOME OWNERSHIP: THE NEW SERFDOM

Low interest rates have made borrowing money easy. That has led to what I've called "flash bubbles" in all kinds of assets—mostly stocks, bonds, and commodities. But it has also affected housing values.

We will soon find out just how durable the housing boom really is. On the face of it, more Americans own homes now than ever before—some 68 percent. But if you dig into the numbers, you see some ugly omens.

First, there was nearly $3.8 trillion in mortgage origination volume in 2003, of which nearly 70 percent was refinancing. The year 2003 was big not just in the volume of mortgages, but also in the percentage of refinancing. For example, in the four quarters starting with Q4 2002, there was a total of $4.2 trillion in total mortgage originations. That was nearly as much as the previous *eight* quarters from Q4 2000 to Q3 2002, during which time there was a total of $4.3 trillion in mortgage activity. And in that eight-quarter period, refinancing activity constituted, on average, less than 50 percent of the market.

Clearly, 2003 was a banner year for refinancing and locking in low rates *before* they began to move up. But in 2004, the incentive of rock-bottom rates began to wane. In April, the Mortgage Bankers Association saw its refinancing index fall 30 percent on a week-over-week basis. That was not long after short-term bond prices cratered—and yields spiked up.

Since then, we've seen an increase in adjustable rate mortgages (ARMs) and a decrease in the percentages of refinancing originations. In plainer terms, once rates started to rise, mortgage activity shifted from healthy borrowers following the incentive of low rates to more inexperienced borrowers, often in the higher-risk or subprime market, taking out riskier adjustable rate loans, and often paying only the interest on those loans.

Why does it matter? These new borrowers are the fuel for home price growth. According to a speech by Federal Reserve Board governor Ed Gramlich, it's the subprime (higher-risk) borrowers that have driven up home ownership rates in America. In prepared remarks delivered to the Financial Services Roundtable meeting in Chicago in May 2004, Gramlich said, "The obvious advantage of the expansion of sub-prime mortgage credit is the rise in credit opportunities and homeownership. Because of innovations in the prime and sub-prime mortgage market, nearly 9 million new homeowners are now able to live in their own homes, improve their neighborhoods, and use their homes to build wealth."[4]

Live in their own homes, maybe. Improve their neighborhoods, perhaps. But build wealth? Only if they can avoid defaulting. And only if housing prices stay high. And only if incomes rise with housing prices to keep prices affordable. First, another quotation from Gramlich's speech: "Subprime borrowers pay higher rates of interest, go into delinquency more often, and have their properties foreclosed at a higher rate than prime borrowers."[5]

Fact, fact, fact. Subprime delinquency rates currently run at around 7 percent, compared to 1 percent with prime mortgages. Still, you might be thinking that is surely not an awful delinquency rate. And surely the benefits of home ownership being dispersed far and wide among Americans is a good thing. It is, after all, the American Dream.

There are risks, though. Delinquency and foreclosure are risks any home owner could run. It simply turns out that the subprime buyers have less margin for error and are therefore more marginal buyers. And it's at the margin—the margin of the entire housing picture—that the subprime buyers begin to become more important.

Gramlich presents us with figures that show subprime mortgage origination rising 25 percent a year for nearly 10 years, between 1994 and 2003. Granted, prime mortgage origination rose at 18 percent a year during the same period. Everybody got in on the cheap money act.

The question today is how dependent growth in home prices is on the demand that's come largely from the subprime market. It's also alarming to note that the latest MBA figures show that adjustable rate mortgages have nearly doubled their percentage of mortgage activity. Why alarming? ARMs with interest-only provisions are a perfect send-up of high-risk borrowers. Such loans look good because the monthly payment (interest only) is typically lower than a fixed-rate loan. But after the period of the fixed rate expires, then the adjustable comes in. Buyers can suddenly face a much higher payment—just to pay the interest. No equity is built. No real ownership is achieved.

Or as Freddie Mac's own chief economist, Frank Nothaft, said, "There is additional risk involved with loans of that type because the family isn't building home equity wealth through amortization of the principal. If the housing market turns weak or dips down, that could put the loan at risk."[6] The unholy marriage of ARMs with subprime borrowers is hardly a foundation of strength on which a new housing rally can be built. But so what? Home purchases are a function of affordability. And even if rates rise and the marginal buyer is wiped out, it's not going to put *everyone* under water.

Well, that's exactly the question. If everyone who refinanced in the last three years sits tight as rates rise, makes payments, and doesn't look to flip or sell the home, then falling home prices won't matter too much, will they? Who cares about liquidity when you're not looking to sell? True. Falling prices hurt less when you're comfortably paying your mortgage. But what happens when you combine falling home prices with rising monthly payments? Danger. Danger.

First, let's look at a sane example. The median price of an existing single-family home in the Midwest is $157,000. Even with increases in monthly payments, buyers of a median home in the Midwest pay only around 15 percent of their income for a mortgage payment. Not a problem.

In the West, however—and, presumably, this is driven by California—the median home price is $275,900. Given the median income in the West, a principal-and-interest monthly mortgage payment on the median home value suddenly eats up 28 percent of a home buyer's income. You don't mind paying nearly 30 percent of your income for your mortgage if (1) your home is going up in value and (2) so is your income. But if your income is flat, as it is for the average American worker, and if *you* are the buyer who's driving home prices up, then paying 30 percent of your income for a home that's falling in market value suddenly becomes . . . less of a good idea.

Now, have I missed something? California has an endless supply of new buyers because of its high population of immigrants. Isn't that enough to sustain rising values? Not if home prices continue to rise faster than income, I say. Won't incomes grow, at least nominally, as inflation takes hold in the economy, erasing the affordability gap? Maybe. Yet even if the liability changes in value (through being paid off in a weaker dollar), the value of the asset may fall, too.

There are a lot of statistical side roads we can wander down, but my main observation is this: Easy money caused home price inflation just as it caused stocks to rise in the 1990s. I'm not saying no one has a right to make money selling a house. But the very idea of home ownership as a means to financial wealth—as Gramlich specifically said—encourages people to treat mortgages not as an asset to amortize, but as a means to speculate on higher home prices. Sure, it can work for a while. But the people who lose the most are always the ones who can least afford to lose anything . . . and get in near the end of the game.

Chapter 2 moves beyond the critical examination of the old economy and presents the first of many strategies you can use to move forward: the exchange-traded fund, or ETF. If you know how mutual funds work, prepare yourself for a fresh, new look at this industry. But before we do that, let's review where America stands at the beginning of the twenty-first century and what the strategic outlook is for bull hunters.

WHAT DOES ALL THIS MEAN?

America is at least $33 trillion in debt. The only real question is whether the money borrowed was used to build factories and income-producing assets or simply wagered on higher financial asset prices. To be sure, some of it was invested rather than gambled away.

But much of this debt was money borrowed to buy other financial assets, namely, stocks and bonds. And that's why you find that the other measure of a financial economy, stock market capitalization as a percentage of GDP, is still dangerously out of whack by all historical standards. By the way, for a great description of how this works, pick up a copy of *Where the Money Grows and Anatomy of the Bubble,* by Garet Garrett (John Wiley, 1997).

Historically, the total market cap of the stock market is about 58 percent of GDP. At the height of the bubble in the Nasdaq, stocks were nearly 185 percent of GDP. That means that while the total value of goods and services in the economy was about $7 trillion, the stock market, on paper at least, was worth $14 trillion. Evidently, the discounted value of America's future earnings was twice as much as the present value. How's that for optimism in the future?

The bear market erased about $7 trillion in stock market wealth before investors counterattacked with the present rally that began in March 2003. Total market cap is about 100 percent of GDP today. In other words, total market cap of around $11 trillion equals total GDP of around $11 trillion. *If stocks returned to their historic average, and did it all at once, you'd see a $4.6 trillion loss in market cap, or a 42 percent decline, from current levels.*

It probably won't happen all at once. But I'm fairly certain it *will* happen. And when it does, it will set unprepared investors back eight years, erasing what they've managed to make up in the last two to three years, and then some. You might be able to afford that, dear reader. And if you can, more power to you. But I can't.

THE DOLLAR, HOUSING, AND DEBT— A TRIPLE THREAT

Your financial future depends on a new approach and, at the very least, an appreciation of the triple threat we face from the dollar, housing, and the national debt. This triple threat assumes that most people will continue investing in the traditional twentieth-century mode.

The threat of a declining dollar, inflated housing values, and growing debt (federal and consumer) are early warning signs that a new strategy is needed. You shouldn't let fear or panic rule your decisions in the markets. But it's good to know the lay of the land before you head out hunting. And as a *bull hunter,* I continue to have faith that bull markets always exist somewhere if we are willing to look for them.

Most investors have a very limited idea of what a bull market is. They think if prices are moving upward, it's a bull market and if prices are moving down, it's a bear market. This is flawed thinking because it's limited thinking. And the world of investment opportunities is anything but limited. Apart from American stocks and bonds, there are other markets with other trends that investors would call bullish and bearish. Yet both kinds of trend can be profitably invested in.

These other trends also directly affect the U.S. dollar. For example, bull markets in energy, raw materials, and China are stronger and more durable than your average cyclical bull market in stocks. That's because they're *not* your average cyclical bull market. Quite the opposite. When you invest in those trends, you're investing in the powerful forces reshaping the global economy.

RESOURCE WARS, ECONOMIC WARS, THE WAR OF IDEAS

After I got back from four months on the road (and three months in Asia), I had a meeting with colleagues in Baltimore, where my publisher is based. I noticed how often the word *war* kept coming up. Of course, I was the one who kept using it. A war over oil. A war over water. A trade war over food and grains.

My point is this. The more you look around today's world, the more you see the economic equivalent of war (total economic warfare, as I've called it), for a simple reason: *More people than ever before are competing for the same scarce resources.*

This competition is what drives bull markets in emerging markets in Asia and across the board in commodities. But any time you have a competition, you have winners and losers. And if the winners are investors who identify the right themes, the losers are investors who stick with the old themes. Contrary to the itchy-fingered compulsion to call a broker and say, "Buy," we need to come to grips with the reality: American stocks are in a long-term bear market. You can chase the rallies, although I recommend doing so only if you can afford to lose the money, and then doing so through options on index and exchange-traded funds.

A more sensible long-term strategy is to identify where prices are moving (either up *or* down) and invest accordingly, regardless of the institutional buy-and-hold, mutual fund bias of the entire investment industry. And what better place to start than with one of the fastest-plummeting investments in the world, the U.S. dollar?

CHAPTER 2

A BULL HUNTER'S SOLUTION TO THE DOLLAR CRISIS

I would as soon leave my son a curse as the almighty dollar.

—Andrew Carnegie[1]

London is famous for its theaters and pubs, but not necessarily its food. Mary Poppins and *The Mousetrap*, yes; mushy peas and jacket potatoes, no. Lately, London is becoming known as a hugely expensive place to live or visit for Americans. In the last two years alone, the dollar has fallen 16 percent against the British pound and by 22 percent against the Australian dollar.

All this probably means very little to you, unless you're in London, for the simple reason that the falling dollar hasn't had much effect on Americans at all—yet. It's true, in theory, that a falling dollar makes imported goods more expensive to buy. But the things most Americans buy don't seem to be getting much more expensive at all, especially cheap electronic goods and textiles from China. "If this is a falling dollar," some Americans say, "let's have a crash!" But before you join them in that sentiment, let me take you through . . .

A DAY IN THE LIFE OF AN OVERSEAS DOLLAR

A typical day in London for me starts with a medium latte at a Starbucks near Covent Garden. It costs £2.39, or about $4.78, according to recent exchange rates. Since I don't typically eat breakfast, my wallet stays unmolested until lunch. A typical lunch, eaten "al desko" as I watch the close of the Asian markets and the futures action in America, is a chicken or ham sandwich, a slice of chocolate cake, maybe some chips (which the English call crisps), and a Coke. Average cost: £5.15, or about $10.30. Dinner is generally not good in England, except in very expensive restaurants. Instead, I might stop for, say, a Guinness at a local pub. This puts me out about £2.85, or about $5.70. Like a good shampoo, the procedure is repeated as many times as necessary or desired.

When you're converting dollars into pounds, you can see that living expenses alone add up very quickly. There are two obvious solutions to my problem. One, don't live in London! That's the simplest of all solutions, and one sure way to reduce my cost of living. The other would be to cut down on expenses. Economize. Adopt the ethic of the English who led the Industrial Revolution. Work hard. Save. Create passive income through investments. This is an important point when you're creating a strategy for dealing with large, macroeconomic events. Focus on the things you can actually do, rather than worrying about events that are completely beyond your control.

But what if suddenly every single city in America became as expensive as London? Imagine waking up and having your cost of living rise by 100 percent while your income stayed absolutely the same. What would that do to your personal finances?

My point is not to scare you to death, although fear is an excellent motivator. But I would like to show you that many of the economic "realities" you take for granted—cheap gasoline, cheap clothes, cheap electronics—*can* change overnight. It's something you should prepare for, even if it doesn't happen, just as you'd prepare for a major winter storm by stocking up on essentials. In this case, your preparation will include finding ways to profit from a falling dollar.

Some of these ways may already be familiar to you. I'll elaborate on them more in coming chapters, but they include buying real assets such as gold, other precious metals, or commodities. Other ways are newer, but no less effective. Not only can they help you soften the blow of big economic forces like the falling dollar, but they can also help you profit from other events like rising (or falling) oil prices, rising (or falling) bond prices, and even purely economic events like slower consumer spending or falling house prices.

DEALING WITH THE DOLLAR

Not all economists agree that currency empires, like the one the dollar has enjoyed since 1973, end with a great inflation. Some investors whom I respect a great deal, such as Bob Prechter and Gary Shilling, believe we're actually headed for deflation whereby cash will be king. But I can't think of any example from history in which a currency empire ended with the currency in question actually gaining in purchasing power. When currencies fall apart, it usually means inflation.

For the record, looking at the world as a bull hunter, I think we'll have both inflation and deflation in the coming years. For the kinds of financial assets I talked about in Chapter 1—most stocks, bonds, and real estate—prices will fall. People won't want to own paper. They'll want to own stuff. For other things, such as commodities or certain kinds of stocks or currencies, there will be a lot *more* demand. People will trade an asset falling in value, the dollar, for something that retains value much better. The Chinese have been doing just this—trading paper for real assets for the last two years. I call this "The Great Resource Grab." In Chapter 6, I'll you what they've been buying and how to benefit.

But I'm getting ahead of myself. It's safe to assume that you wouldn't want to be in a situation where your cost of living doubled or, put another way, your money went half as far as it did the day before. In fact, I'd venture to say you'd do just about anything you could to avoid it. Once you *are* in that situation, you have few good choices. Prices are rising everywhere around you. The money in your wallet that you once thought was, say, as good as gold, turns out to be nothing more than pretty green paper.

This kind of inflation—where it takes more and more money to buy simple things—is a lot more common than you might think. The history books are full of disgraced currencies. I mentioned earlier that it happened to the British pound sterling in 1931. Everyone thought that currency was unsinkable, too—until it sank. It happened to the German reichsmark as well. You can spend a whole hour in the money exhibit at the British Museum looking at pictures of once-valuable currencies that inflated away into worthlessness.

The truth is, currencies come and go only a little less frequently than governments. Good governments do everything they can to create a sound currency. A good government doesn't spend more than it takes in through tax revenues. A good government makes sure tax rates are reasonable enough that reasonable people pay them instead of finding ways to avoid paying them.

You could say that a currency is basically a referendum on the economic health of a country. A country with sound finances and a healthy economy tends to have a sound, or strong, currency. Foreign investors want to own the currency because its value is stable. You can consistently exchange it for goods and services and get real value. Your money has purchasing power.

But if currencies are like beauty pageant contestants, as my friend Dr. Steve Sjuggerud says, then the dollar is currently a big, fat pig with bright red lipstick. Investor Doug Casey calls the dollar "the unbacked liability of a bankrupt government."[2] Jim Rogers says that the dollar is a "deeply flawed currency."[3] All of them are referring to the monstrous debts run up by the U.S. government, which I mentioned in Chapter 1.

By now, you're certain to have heard and read many other bearish statements about the dollar. But the question is, what can you do about it? When Germany experienced hyperinflation in the 1920s, there was little the average German could do, unless he or she owned wealth in some other form—silver dinnerware, for example, or gold jewelry, or even livestock that could be traded for essentials.

Today, the danger to the currency in question (the dollar) is just as great. But here's the good news: *You have far more ways to reduce your dollar risk and make a profit than any other investors in the world have had at a similar economic crisis point.*

In this chapter, I'll show you a few of those choices. And I'll introduce you to an exciting and new way to profit from falling prices that has much less risk than traditional short-selling. It's a classic bull hunter strategy, turning crisis into profits, when most people see only risk. Even if you don't end up using any of these new tools, it's valuable to know that they exist. You can begin thinking about ways to use them in the future.

Right now, bull hunters have a real advantage. Using these new tools will separate you from conventional investors. In a few years, who knows? These new tools may be as popular as mutual funds used to be. If they are, it will be because they offer investors a real solution to a real problem. Right now, one of the biggest problems in the world happens to be the U.S. dollar. Why is that? And, more important, what's the solution?

THE SAFEST PAPER IN THE WORLD

In the years before the U.S. government entered dire financial straits, investors used to want to buy its bonds. In fact, some people— notably, Japanese and Chinese central bankers—*still do.* But more and more investors around the world are beginning to doubt that the U.S. government can keep the trillions of dollars in promises it has made. Those ugly debts and deficits mentioned in Chapter 1 turn out to have real economic consequences. Deficits *do* matter.

The government has made big dollar promises in the Social Security and Medicare programs. It's also made trillions of dollar promises in the form of U.S. bonds, Treasury bills, and Treasury notes held by investors all over the world. These bonds, bills, and notes pay an interest rate. Typically, because the U.S. government has been considered such a low credit risk in the past (very little chance that Uncle Sam would default on his loans or go bankrupt), the interest rate on U.S. government bonds has been lower than on the sovereign bonds issued by governments that are considered more risky.

Keep in mind that the bond is simply a loan you make to the government, which will be paid back with interest over a fixed period of time. As long as the government isn't spending far more than it's taking in through taxes, it doesn't have to borrow too much. But when it makes big promises and spends more and more each year, it has to borrow more and more money. Another way of saying this is that investors have to lend the money to the U.S. government for it to honor its promises to pay.

But what if those investors stop buying U.S. bonds because they realize the U.S. government can't control its spending habits? What would happen to the dollar? More important, how would you know it was about to happen in time for you to *do* something about it?

A DOLLAR DOOMSDAY CLOCK

The more I began to think about this question in the last three years, the more I realized I would have to have some way of knowing what investors thought about the quality of the U.S. government's debt. Did investors still think America's Treasury bonds were the safest investment in the world? Or was news of America's large deficits starting to give investors second thoughts? How could I measure what was going on?

To solve the problem, I invented a new indicator. It's a trip wire of sorts. It tells me when the rest of the world is starting to get nervous about the credit quality of the U.S. government. And here's the important point: *This is another way of telling me what the world thinks about the dollar.*

The less investors like the dollar, the more they're going to demand higher interest payments from the U.S. government. If the interest rate on U.S. bonds isn't good enough to compensate for the dollar risk, investors will sell U.S. bonds and buy someone else's.

If you could compare the interest rates on U.S. bonds to the interest rates on bonds that are considered risky, you'd have a good idea of just how risky the U.S. financial picture is and just how vulnerable the dollar is. In short, to measure dollar risk, you'd need what I call a BEDspread. Once you had it, you'd know when to sell the dollar as it fell or buy it as it rallied.

As I mentioned earlier, U.S. Treasury bonds are widely considered to be the safest investment in the world. The interest rate the government must pay on them reflects the perceived risk by market participants. The 30-year U.S. bond currently yields about 4.67 percent. Uncle Sam is safe, so he doesn't have to pay exorbitant rates of interest to borrow money from you, the government of Japan, or the central planners in Beijing.

On the other hand, so-called *emerging market debt* is perceived as much riskier. In this case, I'm talking about the government bonds of foreign countries like Mexico, Brazil, and Russia. Sometimes you'll hear it called *sovereign debt.* Because all of these governments have had trouble with both their economies and their currencies, they have to pay more to borrow. Their bonds pay investors a higher rate of interest.

The BEDspread—my invention for evaluating dollar risk—is a comparison between rates on U.S. government debt and rates on emerging market debt. By the way, BED stands for "benchmark emerging market debt," which is a mouthful. I've called it *BED* for short and married it to *spread,* or the difference between the interest rate on U.S. bonds and the interest rate on foreign bonds.

I should admit that the BEDspread is biased. As the world recognizes how weak the U.S. government's fiscal situation is, the BEDspread will converge. Uncle Sam will have to pay higher rates of interest to borrow. Foreign governments will pay lower rates as the relative risks between their bonds and American bonds narrow. In other words, American bonds will be recognized as risky. The dollar will fall.

COMPUTING THE SPREAD, EXECUTING THE STRATEGY

Now that you have a way to measure dollar risk, what is it and how can you turn it to your advantage? To measure the yield on U.S. government bonds, I use the Morgan Stanley Government Income Trust closed-end fund (GVT), currently yielding 4.73 percent.

The yield on GVT is slightly different from the yield on the 30-year bond because GVT is a basket of U.S. debt of different types and maturities. For example, 38 percent of GVT's holdings are in Treasury bonds, 23 percent in Fannie Mae bonds, and 19.6 percent in other U.S. agency bonds. All together, GVT is an excellent proxy for the creditworthiness (or risk) of the American government.

To measure the yield on emerging market debt, I use the Salomon Brothers Emerging Markets Income Fund (EMD). This is a basket of sovereign emerging market debt. For example, 23 percent of the fund's holdings are in Brazilian bonds, 18 percent in Russian bonds, and 16.5 percent in Mexican bonds. The average yield at the time we go to press is 8.84 percent.

To get the BEDspread, you simply subtract GVT's yield from EMD's yield. Based on recent closing prices, I calculated the BEDspread at 4.11 percent. That's well under 5 percent, where the spread was the previous spring. But it's also 73 basis points *tighter* than it was three months prior.

The spread changes a little bit every day. What you're looking for is the general trend over time. That trend has clearly been toward higher yields on U.S. government bonds and lower yields on foreign government bonds. If my formula is designed well, the narrowing spread should show a falling dollar in that time. Does it? Take a look at Figure 2.1.

As you can see, as the BEDspread has narrowed, the dollar *has* fallen. Figure 2.1 shows the U.S. Dollar Index. It tracks the performance of the dollar against a basket of foreign currencies, mainly the euro. If the relationship holds, the narrower the spread gets, the more the dollar will fall. Someday—perhaps sooner than most investors think possible—the spread will actually converge and the dollar will utterly collapse. It's not a cheerful prospect—unless you can do something about it.

Of course, it's not meant to be cheerful. It's meant to be helpful at dispelling persistent illusions about the soundness of the dollar and America's finances. As you know, illusions often die a sudden and not-so-respectable death. For example, one day on the Paris metro, not long before I came up with the BEDspread, I found myself standing next to an overweight and slightly smelly middle-aged woman. She took to the center of the car and began chanting under her breath *Pere Noel est morte* ("Santa Claus is dead"). This was a few weeks before Christmas. While the death of Santa Claus was not news to me (nor was it exactly true, in the sense that Santa Claus is a

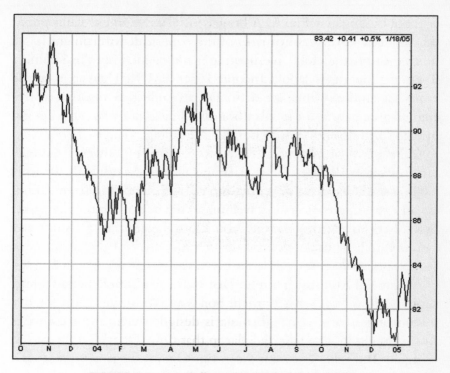

FIGURE 2.1 U.S. Dollar Index (End of Day) ($USD).
(Source: © 2004 DecisionPoint.com)

noble idea that persists), it was quite shocking to all the children on the train who could hear the woman and were scared of her to begin with. You could say a crash in the Santa index ensued.

Such is the fate of misplaced faith, which brings us to the dollar. The BEDspread is really your private measure of how close we are to total financial meltdown. It's a measure of *systemic risk.* It's premised on the belief that the U.S. bond market is the financial world's safe haven of last resort. But that belief turns out to be, to borrow a phrase from Michael Moore, a big fat lie. But it's a lie we can profit from.

GOING SHORT U.S. BONDS

If you want to profit from the dollar's decline, or its occasional coun-tertrend rallies, you have to know how to invest in U.S. bonds—

without buying or selling U.S. bonds. Just five years ago you couldn't do this. But now, thanks to new exchange-traded funds and index funds, you can go long or short U.S. bonds as simply as buying a stock. Following is a fuller explanation of what exchange-traded funds are and how they work. Chapter 3 will give you three more examples of how you can use them. But here, I want to focus on just one opportunity: making money off the falling dollar.

Take a look at Figure 2.2. It shows the two bull market channels for an exchange-traded fund with the ticker symbol TLT. The full name is the iShares 20-year+ Treasury Bond Fund. In plainer terms, it's an exchange-traded fund that tracks the performance of a basket of U.S. bonds. It turns the entire U.S. bond market into a stock you can buy, sell, or trade, depending on your view of the market and your appetite for risk.

Figure 2.2 has some interesting technical features. I've drawn lines on it to show you what I mean. It shows two distinct times when bond prices have risen. The most recent rally starts to lose technical steam around 92—exactly the place the last bond market rally ran out of steam. But what does this mean fundamentally? And what does it mean for the dollar?

FIGURE 2.2 As bond prices fall, interest rates will rise.

If I am right about the dollar, TLT will collapse. Specifically, bond prices will fall as U.S. interest rates rise and the dollar collapses. The last time we had a great inflation in the United States, bond yields went to the high teens as the dollar crumbled and Americans waited for hours in gas lines. If the same type of thing were to happen today, TLT could fall quickly, and I mean fall hard. It would go below 89, breaking the upward price channel and heading much lower as bond yields rise. An investor would want to be short TLT in that case. Or even better, an options buyer would own put options (see Chapter 4 for a discussion of call and put options). But let's say I'm wrong about the dollar. What would happen to bond prices and what could you do about it?

BULLISH DOLLAR SCENARIOS

If the dollar rallies (as some commentators think it will), then bond prices may actually rise and interest rates will stay low! I find this very unlikely, mainly because I think America's large deficits are an albatross around the neck of the bond market. But as a bull hunter, I don't particularly care what happens, only that I have a way to profit from it. Up, down, sideways—the main thing is to profit.

On a dollar rally, you could go long or buy TLT, just like you'd buy a stock. And there are many other ETF options. For example, there's IEF, which is the ticker symbol for the iShares Lehman 10-year Treasury bond fund. It's another bond fund ETF that tracks bonds of shorter maturity, usually 10 years plus. Incidentally, the IEF chart is remarkably similar to the TLT chart—two different ways to invest in the same strategy.

There are other good bond market proxies, too. One is AGG, which is a basket of *all* government bonds, not just Treasury bonds. If you want to be short the entire U.S. government, you can. Or if you want to buy bonds but not use government bonds, you could buy LQD. That's the ticker symbol for the Goldman Sachs corporate bond fund. It's a basket of corporate bonds that trades like a single stock.

One of the great benefits of ETFs is transparency. You can know precisely what you're buying (or selling?). For example, check out Table 2.1; I pulled it off the ishares.com site just now to find out what bonds are basketed up in LQD. In the next section, I'll show you some other benefits of ETFs and why they're different (and superior) to mutual funds.

There are other ways to hedge against a fall in the U.S. dollar. You can buy gold, for example. Gold is a kind of antidollar. Or you could buy put options on the U.S. dollar index shown in Figure 2.1. This is a little more complicated because it means buying options on futures. You could also simply open a bank account in a foreign country like Canada and deposit your savings there. I'll talk about that and other strategies for the future in Chapter 9.

For now, I like using ETFs to deal with threats like the dollar or opportunities like crude oil. ETFs are easy to use, have many benefits, and are becoming more and more popular with investors for these and other reasons. In fact, let's take a look at the world of ETFs in greater detail.

Mutual Funds	*ETFs*
They are bought and sold directly through fund management.	They are more liquid: They are traded on the exchange just like stocks.
They are diversified by investment goal, objective, or risk level.	They are diversified among a basket of stocks by sector or country.
There is no provision for short-selling or margin buying; options are not allowed.	They can be sold short or bought on margin; options are available on many ETFs.
Fees can be high and many are not visible.	Fees to investors are as low as 1 percent.
Investors have no easy means to know what the fund has in its portfolio.	ETF portfolios are completely transparent; investors always know what they own.
The portfolio is intact and controlled by fund management.	In some cases, ETF holdings can be broken apart by investors.

TABLE 2.1 A BASKET OF CORPORATE BONDS
AS OF 1/14/2005

Top Holdings* (Daily)

Name	Coupon	Maturity	Rating (Moody's/S&P)	% of Fund
1 AT&T Broadband Corp.	9.45	11/15/2022	Baa3/BBB	1.32%
2 Sprint Cap Corp.	8.75	3/15/2032	Baa3/BBB–	1.28%
3 Devon Energy Corp.	7.95	4/15/2032	Baa2/BBB	1.23%
4 Verizon Global FDG C	7.75	12/1/2030	A2/A+	1.19%
5 AT&T Broadband Corp.	8.38	3/15/2013	Baa3/BBB	1.18%
6 AOL Time Warner Inc.	7.70	5/1/2032	Baa1/BBB+	1.16%
7 Weyerhaeuser Co.	7.38	3/15/2032	Baa2/BBB	1.15%
8 France Telecom S.A.	8.50	3/1/2011	Baa2/BBB+	1.15%
9 General Elec Cap Corp.	6.75	3/15/2032	Aaa/AAA	1.13%
10 AT&T Wireless Svcs. I	7.88	3/1/2011	Baa2/A	1.13%

Top Sectors/Industries

Sector/Industry	% of Fund
1 Financials	40.14%
2 Consumer	26.95%
3 Industrials	15.31%
4 Telecom and Technology	14.31%
5 Utilities	2.06%

*Holdings are subject to change.
Source: iShares.com

A WORLD OF PROFITS IS POSSIBLE USING ETFS

Exchange-traded funds, what I call *precision-guided investments* (PGIs), have enormous profit potential. PGIs offer more diversification than single stocks, lower expenses than mutual funds, and most important, complete trading flexibility—including options (you'll read about that later). And with over 130 ETFs available in the United States today, you have a whole world of investment choices. As you come to understand ETFs better, not only will you be able to cash in big on the options plays, but you can also wave good-bye to those high-cost, underperforming, and scandal-plagued mutual funds forever.

In just 10 short years, this new PGI weapon has grown from obscurity into one of the most powerful tools a trader has. Yet trading volumes for these potent instruments are only just now starting to grow. Learning how to deploy them for investment profits as they become even more popular is the key to getting in on this new and lucrative market.

First, we have to define *precision-guided investment*. Imagine a single security that allows you to buy an entire sector or industry or even country—in just one stock. It gives you all the benefits of single stocks (all-day trading, margin buying, short-selling, and options trading). But because you're buying a basket of stocks, you don't have the risk of owning a single stock that may have a bad earnings report, an accounting scandal, or some other unexpected negative news. And imagine owning a powerful investment idea that can deliver you leveraged returns—without paying big management fees.

A NEW WORLD OF TRADING POWER

ETFs are a cross between individual stocks and index mutual funds, and they offer the best of both worlds—and then some. Each ETF is a basket of stocks. These baskets track anything from a broad-based market index to a designated country to a pinpointed economic sector. This ability to own a lot of stocks in a single instrument, though, is where the similarity to mutual funds ends. Like individual stocks, ETFs offer trading flexibility:

- All-day trading, every day
- Options trading (on selected ETFs)
- Short-selling
- Margin buying

ETFs have even more beneficial features, such as transparency (meaning you can see everything they're holding all the time). In the preceding example, it means you can see exactly what corporate bonds LQD is holding. For most other ETFs, it will be a list of stocks and industries. I'll show you some examples in Chapter 3. ETFs also offer low fees. (How does less than 1 percent sound to you?) If actively managed ETFs debut soon, the fees will probably go up. Until then, the ETFs also offer a tax efficiency that you can't get from individual stocks or traditional mutual funds.

On their own, ETFs offer a unique investing opportunity. They become a truly powerful way to safely—and significantly—increase your personal wealth. ETFs enhance your portfolio in two important ways:

1. They offer the opportunity to invest in specific securities for a capital gain.
2. The low fees and tax efficiency preserve your gains—unlike more traditional investment options, where you can lose a significant portion of your earnings to fees and taxes.

This one-two ETF punch can build your wealth in a way not available with any other security.

THE SEVEN MONEYMAKING FEATURES OF ETFS

ETFs incorporate the seven features of a profitable investment. With a brief look at each feature, you'll learn why ETFs should become the mainstay of your winning portfolio.

1. *Risk diversification:* ETFs let you buy an entire market, sector, or country with a single stocklike investment. For example, if you believe the Singapore economy is set to grow, you could invest in a Singapore index fund—and eliminate the guesswork of trying to pick the one or two "right" companies. You still own a focused investment (Singapore), *and* you get the profit potential of a single stock. But because ETFs hold a basket of securities, you're protected against the risks inherent in any single holding.

2. *Index tracking:* Passive management—an innate feature of index ETFs—removes manager risk from your portfolio, further stabilizing your investment. With index tracking, you don't bear the risk that a fund manager will make a bad investment choice.

3. *All-day trading:* ETFs allow you to buy and sell anytime the markets are open. That means you'll always have up-to-the-minute pricing—not like with mutual funds that post net asset value (NAV) prices only at the market close.

4. *Strategic trading capability:* Stop orders . . . limit orders . . . short-selling . . . margin buying . . . ETFs offer you a wide variety of trading choices. You have complete flexibility—something no mutual fund can offer. Plus, many ETFs give you options-trading capability and the increased profit potential that goes along with that. Finally, most ETFs don't have any minimum investment or round-lot requirements—meaning you can invest $50 and even buy single units.

5. *Tax efficiency:* ETFs, like index mutual funds, are passively managed—meaning less buying and selling within the fund. Less trading means fewer capital gains distributions—and that translates into lower taxes for you. And ETFs also give you a way to save taxes that mutual funds just can't: Mutual fund holders have to purchase and redeem shares directly from the fund, which can cause capital gains distributions to all shareholders. But ETFs trade over an exchange, so transactions affect only a single shareholder.

6. *Lowest fees:* ETFs sport the lowest fees going—almost always less than 1 percent, but sometimes going as low as 0.09 percent. No mutual fund going can beat that!

7. *Transparent holdings:* You can view ETF portfolio holdings 24/7—unlike mutual funds, which are required to disclose their holdings only twice a year.

In short, you get focus, flexibility, efficiency, and diversification all in one investment. Add those key benefits to increased profit potential—without increased risk—and you get what amounts to a practically perfect addition to any portfolio.

THE HAZARDS OF INDIVIDUAL STOCKS

Why not just buy stocks directly? Sometimes I recommend doing so, *if* I'm convinced it's a good business at a reasonable price with a strong fundamental trend behind it. But when you buy stock in a single company, you expose your portfolio to an additional layer of investment risk. Sometimes that risk is well worth it. If you can get a good business at a good price, that's a fair risk. But part of becoming a bull hunter is branching out into other opportunities, even if they're new and unfamiliar. What matters is whether they work.

Regardless of how well the markets are performing, how strong the economy is, how in favor a sector becomes, any single stock is riddled with the risk of becoming worthless. There could be a management scandal (think Enron and Tyco), there could be infighting (think Disney), the company could get socked with a serious lawsuit (like Microsoft), the CEO could be in a plane crash, the company could file for bankruptcy . . . any of these events could send a stock into a downward spiral—and your wealth along with it.

Buying a whole sector, a whole country, a whole index eliminates that risk. Even if one company in the basket goes bust, the rest of the holdings will remain on track.

LEARNING THE ETF LANGUAGE

Most stock investors know the differences between common and preferred stock; with the ETF market, you need to master a few new terms as part of the learning curve. ETFs come in two major categories: index and closed-end. Our primary focus is on index ETFs. Among them, they track a wide variety of sector-specific, country-specific, and broad-market indexes—and use a lot of acronyms. These include the following:

- SPDRs, or Standard & Poor's Depository Receipts (SPY), as they're formally known, were the first publicly traded ETF. SPDRs track the S&P 500 Index; baby SPDRs track subsectors of the index. For example, the Energy SPDR (XLE) tracks (you guessed it) energy companies, like those focused on crude oil and natural gas; the Technology SPDR holds companies involved with computers and peripherals, IT providers, telecommunications, and so on.
- Diamonds (DIA) is the nickname for the Dow Diamonds, an ETF that holds all the stocks that make up the Dow Jones Industrial Average, which includes heavy hitters like Coca-Cola, IBM, and Wal-Mart.
- Qubes (QQQ) tracks the 100 stock index, which focuses on the most actively traded stocks on Nasdaq, making it essentially a technology index. Not surprisingly, QQQ is the most heavily traded ETF. It trades on the American Exchange (Amex).
- iShares is the ETF family backed by Barclay's Global Investors. This group offers a wide variety of ETFs to choose from, including international indexes (such as its Emerging Markets ETF), market sectors (like telecommunications), and broad-market indexes (like the Russell 3000).
- HOLDRs, although similar to standard ETFs, add an unusual twist: This basket of stocks can be unbundled, so you can trade the underlying stocks individually. Each HOLDR (or Holding Company Depository Receipt) is initially made up of about 20

stocks in the same sector; should events (like a merger) knock one out of the bucket, there's no replacement.

Regardless of its acronym, each ETF sticks to the same basic rule: When you invest in an ETF, you know what you're getting. There are no hidden fees or hidden agendas. If you buy a tech-stock-based ETF, it will hold only tech stocks—and you'll know exactly which ones all the time. Plus, as you'll see in Chapter 3, they provide an excellent way to trade major investment themes, such as the falling dollar, the Asian commodities boom, or volatile crude oil markets.

That's a short introduction to ETFs. Following is a list of some of the more well-known ones. But every day more are coming. ETFs on China and gold came out in 2004. They became convenient ways for investors to be long or short two of the biggest investment themes of the year. Maybe someday soon you'll even be able to buy options on them. Think of that! You could put calls on China or puts on gold, or puts on China and calls on gold.

Some index funds and ETFs already make it possible to trade options. But that's a different subject, which I'll cover later. The good news is that there are new tools called exchange-traded funds that make it possible to turn virtually any idea into a profitable investment opportunity. You now have the ability to turn what used to be an unavoidable risk into a profitable event.

This is what I mean about seeing things like a bull hunter. Yes, the prospect of a collapsing dollar is scary. It should be taken seriously and prepared for seriously. For that, we'll cover other opportunities in Chapters 7 and 8. But converting a big risk like the falling dollar into a very real and simple-to-realize investment opportunity is one of the characteristics of the world you now live in. You're free to pass up the opportunity.

But I hope to show you in the next few chapters that it's much simpler, cheaper, and more effective than you might expect. As John F. Kennedy put it, "When written in Chinese, the word *crisis* is composed of two characters. One represents danger and the other represents opportunity."[4] We've looked at one crisis in this chapter. Now, let's look at three opportunities. In Chapter 3 you'll see how to use ETFs to achieve a remarkably large list of investment objectives.

American Stock Exchange (Amex) Indexes

Amex Airline Index (XAL)

Amex Biotechnology Index (BTK)

Amex Computer Technology Index (XCI)

Amex Defense Index (DFI)

Amex Disk Drive Index (DDX)

Amex Hong Kong Option Index (HKO)

Amex Japan Index (JPN)

Amex Major Market Index (XMI)

Amex Natural Gas Index (XNG)

Amex Oil Index (XOI)

Amex Pharmaceutical Index (DRG)

Amex Securities Broker/Dealer Index (XBD)

Credit Suisse First Boston Technology Index (CTN)

Deutsche Bank Energy Index (DXE)

Ftse EUROTOP 100 Index (EUR)

Inter@ctive Week Internet Index (IIX)

CBOE Mini-NDX Index (MNX)

Morgan Stanley Commodity-Related Index (CRX)

Morgan Stanley Consumer Index (CMR)

Morgan Stanley Internet Index (MOX)

Morgan Stanley Technology Index (MSH)

Morgan Stanley Retail Index (MVR)

Morgan Stanley Biotech Index (MVB)

Morgan Stanley Oil Services (MGO)

Nasdaq Biotechnology Index (NBI)

Nasdaq 100 Index (NDX)

S&P Midcap 400 (MID)

Broad-Based, CBOE Sector, and Dow Jones Index Options
(Listed on Chicago Board Options Exchange)

CBOE Asia 25 Index (EYR)

CBOE Euro 25 Index (EOR)

CBOE Mexico Index (MEX)

Dow Jones Industrial Average (DJX)

Dow Jones Industrial Average LEAPS (ticker symbol varies with expiration month)

S&P 100 Index (OEX)

S&P 100 Euro-Style Index (XEO)

S&P 500 Index (SPX)

S&P Long-Dated (SPL)

S&P Small-Cap 600 Index (SML)

Goldman Sachs Technology Index (GTC)

NYSE Composite Index (NYA)

Russell 2000 Index (RUT)

Morgan Stanley Multinational Company Index (NFT)

CBOE Gold Index (GOX)

CBOE Internet Index (INX2)

CBOE Oil Index (OIX)

CBOE Technology Index (TXX)

Dow Ten Index (MUT)

HOLDRs Listed on the American Stock Exchange

Biotech HOLDRs (BBH)

Broadband HOLDRs (BDH)

B2B Internet HOLDRs (BHH)

Europe 2001 HOLDRs (EKH)

Internet HOLDRs (HHH)

Internet Architecture HOLDRs (IAH)

Internet Infrastructure HOLDRs (IIH)

Market 2000+ HOLDRs (MKH)

Oil Service HOLDRs (OIH)

Pharmaceutical HOLDRs (PPH)

Regional Bank HOLDRs (RKH)

Retail HOLDRs (RTH)

Semiconductor HOLDRs (SMH)

Software HOLDRs (SWH)

Telecom HOLDRs (TTH)

Utilities HOLDRs (UTH)

Wireless HOLDRs (WMH)

Exchange-Traded Funds

Fortune 500 Index Tracking Stock (FFF)

Fortune e-50 Index Tracking Stock (FEF)

iShares Dow Jones U.S. Financial Sector (IYF)

iShares Dow Jones U.S. Technology (IYW)

iShares Dow Jones U.S. Telecommunications (IYZ)

iShares Nasdaq Biotechnology (IBB)

iShares Russell 1000 (IWB)

iShares Russell 1000 Growth (IWF)

iShares Russell 1000 Value (IWD)

iShares Russell 2000 (IWM)

iShares Russell 2000 Growth (IWO)

iShares Russell 2000 Value (IWN)

iShares Russell 3000 (IWV)

iShares S&P 100 Index Fund (OEF)

CHAPTER 3

ETF STRATEGIES IN ACTION

A human being should be able to change a diaper, plan an invasion, butcher a hog, conn a ship, design a building, write a sonnet, balance accounts, build a wall, set a bone, comfort the dying, take orders, give orders, cooperate, act alone, solve equations, analyze a new problem, pitch manure, program a computer, cook a tasty meal, fight efficiently, and die gallantly. Specialization is for insects.

—Robert A. Heinlein[1]

In the fall of 2002 I gave a speech that was not well received by the audience. The speech warned against the coming fall in the dollar. It also warned about the dangers of deficit spending. The strongest warnings, however, were that a long, sustained war on terrorism was a threat to your financial freedom and, eventually, your liberty.

There were a few people who listened, though, and liked it. One of them came up to me afterward. She and her husband were living a comfortable life in northern California. He was a programmer in Silicon Valley. She sold real estate. She was worried about the issues I brought up.

Two years later, I wrote to readers of my investment newsletter, *Strategic Investment,* that I was about to spend three months in Asia doing investment research for what would become the book you're reading right now. Dozens of them wrote back, inviting me to their homes and businesses in Japan, China, India, Australia, and Thailand. I took many of them up on their generous offers. It gave me valuable insight on each country from people who were actually living and investing in the places I wanted to write about. One of the e-mails proved fortuitous:

Dear Dan,

You may not remember me. But several years ago I heard you speak at the Agora Wealth Symposium in San Francisco. I just wanted to let you know that since then, my husband and I have moved to Thailand! We took your dollar warning seriously and we also wanted a change in our quality of life. We now run a mountain bike rental bicycle shop on the island of Koh Samui in the Gulf of Siam. When we're not running our business, we're managing our investments reading *Strategic Investment* and the *Daily Reckoning.* We'd love to see you when you're in Thailand and show off our little slice of paradise and tell you what we think of investing in this country.

How could I turn down an offer like that? I am an avid mountain biker. What's more, I'd get a chance to talk with real readers about how they were personally dealing with the investment challenges I wrote about every day.

Not everyone will choose to move to Thailand as a hedge against the falling dollar, though some have. Many others have set up bank accounts or established second homes outside the United States. These are large, quality-of-life decisions that I think it's healthy to at least consider.

But as you saw in Chapter 2, you already have at your disposal a broad arsenal of remarkably diverse investment weapons to deal with the world's many threats and its many more opportunities. The risk of a crashing dollar merits the consideration of what others would call radical alternatives. But there are many less radical choices you can make to achieve similar results. I'll give you three examples in this chapter.

It's possible, of course, that I'm wrong about many of my big-picture predictions. Although my track record over the last four years has been pretty good, you are either wrong or right about the collapse of a currency. There is not a lot of middle ground. But as a bull hunter, you must remember that your goal is to find the big trends and then find the best tools for investing in them.

The trend may be up or it may be down. It may be in commodities or currencies. It may be in U.S. tech stocks or Australian mining stocks. But the unique advantage of using ETFs is that you can invest in all these trends quickly and easily, wherever they might be and whichever direction they might be going. There is no trick to it. But you have to think as a bull hunter, not as a "buy and hold" investor.

It's a small change in thinking. But it's the kind of change that allows you to *do* more. It allows you to invest in different sectors, different asset classes, and even different countries all over the globe. As the quotation from Robert Heinlein at the beginning of this chapter says, "Specialization is for insects." You do not want to invest like an insect these days, as a specialist. It will doom you to certain poor performance, if not outright extinction. And with the existence of so many new ways to make money from so many different markets, there's no good reason not to at least consider some ETF strategies in action.

AN AMERICAN MELT-UP?

If you polled them, you'd find that the 30,000 readers of my newsletter, *Strategic Investment,* are unlikely to associate the word *bullish* with my investment views. After all, I'm predicting that certain financial stocks will lose up to 90 percent of their market capitalization in the next few years. But as an investor, you should always be more concerned with making money than being right about your favorite ideas.

All my analysis tells me I will be right about the dollar. And all my preparation allows me to profit if I am. You can profit as well, as I've shown you. But you can also prepare and profit if the Dow Jones goes to infinity and beyond! You simply have to find the best way to profit if stocks—unlikely as it seems to me—are about to embark on a powerful bull market.

There are plenty of smart people who think that the next 20 years will be even better for investors than the last 20 years. "Put it right between your eyes," said Ken Fisher at a *Money Week* Roundtable I attended in London. "The fundamentals are in place in the American economy for a huge melt *up* in the stock market."[2]

Money Week is a weekly financial journal published in London to which I often contribute my views. Every six weeks, its editor, Merryn Somerset Webb, holds an informal roundtable discussion about the market. She invites brokers, analysts, bankers, and when they're visiting London, American stock market pundits like Ken Fisher.

Fisher's prediction prompted me to formalize the strategies I'd been developing for ETFs. ETFs are growing fast, but they're fairly new. Most of my work in them up to that point was trading options on them. (You'll read more about that in Chapter 4.)

But it's possible—and even advisable—to use ETFs to participate in the clear market themes of the day. For example, some patient research will tell you which sector of the American stock market would do the best in Fisher's "American melt-up" scenario. Once you identified the sector, you could then pick the three or four best stocks in the sector, buy them, and hope for the best.

This is just what many investors did in the technology bull market from 1998 and 2000. They bought stocks like Lucent, Microsoft, Cisco, Amazon, Intel, and Qualcomm and never looked back. Some of them *did* get rich. But many of them did not. Even today, four years after the tech crash, the most actively traded stocks in the market are *still* the tech bellwethers of 2000. Many investors still own them and are still trying to sell them.

This is the risk you run in buying individual stocks. You can be right about the idea (a bull market in technology) but buy the wrong stock. Or you can be right about the idea and end up buying a company that runs afoul of the law with accounting "irregularities." Don't get me wrong. I still recommend individual stocks. But only if

I'm convinced that I'm buying a good company that I thoroughly understand, and I'm buying it at a good price.

A better way to invest in a hypothetical second coming of the bull market is to identify the leading sectors and invest in *them* rather than trying to find the leading stocks. If you're a savvy investor, maybe you'll be good enough to identify that one company that's going to do a thousand percent better than all the others. Modesty, however, is a good investment virtue to have. And with exchange-traded funds, you can be both modest *and* ambitious.

LEADING THE MARKET UP

When all stocks are rising in what conventional investors would call a bull market, there are certain stocks that do better than others. Small company stocks do very well because they are *growth* stocks. They can grow their sales and earnings faster than large companies. Plus, there are thousands available. What investor does not salivate at the prospect of being one of the few visionaries who buys a company that starts in a garage and turns it into a multi-billion-dollar global empire?

Then there are technology stocks. Technology, its advocates will tell you, is dynamic. It makes the world more productive. It turns a slow, dirty, smokestack economy into a fast, clean, knowledge economy. When you use new telecommunications technology in your business to increase productivity, you create additional profits without incurring additional cost. You do more with less because you have better tools.

Doing more with less because you have better tools is precisely the principle of using ETFs. If small stocks and technology stocks "lead the market up" during broad bull markets, wouldn't the best strategy be to buy as many small-capitalization and technology stocks as possible? It would be if you could afford it. But buying 20 stocks means paying 20 different share prices, paying 40 different commissions (once when you buy and once when you sell), tracking 20 different investments, and most important, taking on 20 different risks.

Why bother with all that when you can take on just two risks and own all the best small-cap stocks in the market along with all the best technology stocks in the market? If you're wrong about the big trend in the market, you have only 2 risks instead of 10 or 20. If you're right, you profit directly from the best-performing stocks.

A SMALL-CAP STRATEGY

The Russell 2000 is an index of small-cap stocks. The index is designed to tell investors how small-cap stocks are doing as a group. It makes it easier to compare small caps to say, the Dow 30 or the S&P 500. Because small-cap stocks are often growth stocks and highly volatile, they can be a leading indicator of a broader rally in all stocks. From a business perspective, it also makes sense. Small firms are at the front lines of the economy. They are the most sensitive to changes in business conditions. When the economy is growing, small firms see it and profit from it first. That's why investors love to scoop up small-cap shares at the end of a recession. They know that small-cap stocks will rise as the fortunes of small-cap companies improve.

What you may not know is that you can buy all 2000 stocks on the Russell 2000 . . . in one single stock. Let me introduce you to IWM, or what is formally known as the iShares Russell 2000 Index Fund.

IWM tracks the Russell 2000. When you buy IWM, you are essentially buying the performance of the Russell 2000, much as when you buy the triple Qs, you're buying the performance of the top 100 Nasdaq stocks. Figure 3.1 shows you that IWM does clearly track the Russell 2000 (RUT). This is an important correlation to look for. You want to make sure the ETF you're buying actually imitates the performance of the index or underlying commodity it's designed to track. You can do so by constructing a chart that resembles Figure 3.1 or, more easily, by consulting the prospectus of the ETF you're looking at. As you can also see from Figure 3.1, in the large market rally that began in the spring of 2003, both IWM and RUT have clearly outperformed the Dow, leading the market up.

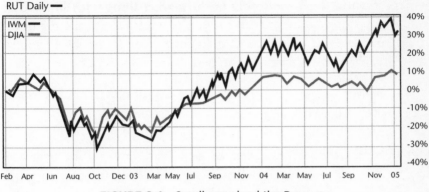

FIGURE 3.1 Small caps lead the Dow up.

It's nice to know your theory of small caps leading the market up is correct. But another benefit of ETFs is that you always know what's in the basket of stocks you bought. You can view individual holdings and see them broken down into sectors. I'll tell you why this is important in just a moment. But first, look at Table 3.1. This shows you the top 10 holdings in IWM and the top 10 sectors and industries the individual holdings fall into.

Knowing what you own isn't just a convenience. It's essential. With ETFs, you always know what you own. That means you also know what you're buying before you've ever spent a dime—something that's not always true with mutual funds. It's a good idea to check what an ETF's holdings are. For an ETF like IWM, it's easy. The ETF has the same holdings as the stocks in the underlying index, in this case the Russell 2000. The same is true for other index ETFs.

But not all ETFs are index ETFs. In fact, as they become more possible, you can expect more ETFs that slice the market into smaller ideas. If you're a precision-guided investor, this is good news. It means that for virtually any investment idea or theme you have, you'll be able to find an ETF that matches it. You'll have a simple way to directly benefit from your idea, without the risk of buying just one single stock. However with the variety of offerings comes the burden of deciding which one to buy.

TABLE 3.1   A BASKET OF THE BEST SMALL CAPS

Top Holdings* (Daily)		Top Sectors/Industries	
1 New Century Financial Corp. REIT	0.22%	1 Financial services	23.63%
2 Goodyear Tire & Rubber Co.	0.21%	2 Consumer discretionary	18.26%
3 Laidlaw International Inc.	0.21%	3 Health care	12.06%
4 Landstar System Inc.	0.20%	4 Technology	12.05%
5 Terex Corp.	0.20%	5 Materials and processing	10.27%
6 Penn National Gaming Inc.	0.20%	6 Producer durables	7.69%
7 Crown Holdings Inc.	0.20%	7 Other energy	5.02%
8 Energen Corp.	0.20%	8 Auto and transportation	4.38%
9 Valeant Pharmaceuticals International	0.19%	9 Utilities	4.34%
10 Joy Global Inc.	0.19%	10 Consumer staples	1.59%

*Holdings are subject to change.
Source: iShares.com

BUY THE INTERNET WITH JUST ONE STOCK

Internet and technology stocks have also led the market up in the recent past. Personally, I think this has more to do with the low interest rates making it easy to borrow money and buy speculative stocks. But my opinion does not stand in the way of the facts. If tech stocks lead the market up, ETFs make it possible for you to buy the leading tech stocks in smaller baskets.

Take a look at Figure 3.2, which shows the performance of two popular technology-oriented baskets. One is a basket of wireless stocks (WMH); the other is a basket of Internet stocks (HHH). Figure 3.2 compares the performance of both to the Dow 30 over the last three years. As you can see, HHH not only clobbered the Dow almost 10 to 1, it did the same to WMH. There was a time when wireless stocks were big news—in the media, that is. And you

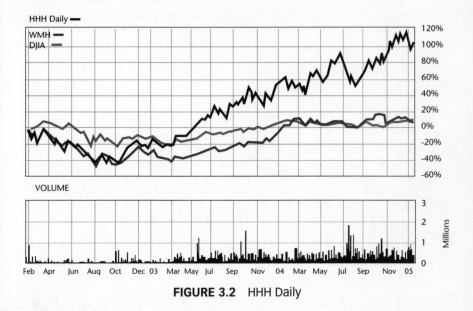

FIGURE 3.2 HHH Daily

can see there were a few periods when WMH screamed up, only to give back ground later. You can see in Table 3.2 that WMH is made up of 21 different wireless stocks. In this case, each stock has a different weighting that affects the performance of the whole basket. As you can see, WMH does *not* correlate with conventional bull markets. That doesn't mean there aren't ways to still profit from it—especially those spikes up and down. I'll show you how to do that in Chapter 4.

But if you do a little homework, you can see that HHH is a far better way to invest in the American melt-up idea. It's like buying the entire Internet in just one stock. As always, you can see exactly what stocks are in HHH's basket. And as you can see, they are some of the most well-known names doing business, and sometimes even making money, on the Internet. When investors are bullish on the Internet, these are the stocks they feel comfortable buying. See Table 3.3.

There are only 13 stocks in HHH. But they happen to be 13 stocks that lead powerful bull market rallies. You could buy just one of them, a few of them, or each and every one. But in each case,

TABLE 3.2   BUYING THE WIRELESS WORLD IN ONE STOCK

Stock	Ticker
Aether Systems, Inc.	AETH
AT&T Corp.—AT&T Wireless Group	AWE
Crown Castle International Corp.	CCI
Deutsche Telecom AG ADS	DT
Ericsson LM Telephone Company	ERICY
Freescale Semiconductor Inc.	FDL.B
Motorola, Inc.	MOT
Nextel Communications Inc.	NXTL
Nextel Partners, Inc.	NXTP
Nokia Corp.	NOK
Qualcomm Inc.	QCOM
Research in Motion Ltd.	RIMM
RF Micro Devices, Inc.	RFMD
S R Telecom	SRXA
SK Telecom Co., Ltd.	SKM
Sprint Corporation—PCS Group	FON
Telesp Celular Participaceos S.A.	TCP
Verizon Communications	VZ
Vodafone Group p.l.c.	VOD
United States Cellular Corp.	USM
Western Wireless Corp.	WWCA

Source: Amex.com

you'd have a different risk. Buy the wrong one, and you miss the overall gain. Buy a few of them, and you spend a lot of money and may again not get the large overall blended gain. Buy them all individually, and you are probably already rich, so have as much fun as you can afford!

Or buy them all as one single stock through HHH. You buy the hottest sector during a bull market. You haven't eliminated your risk. You never do. An ETF can go down just like a stock can. But if you're right, you've picked the single best way to profit from the hot sector with the least risk. And the news gets better! Not only is it

**TABLE 3.3   THE EASIEST WAY TO BUY
(OR TRADE) THE INTERNET**

Stock	Ticker	Share Amount
Amazon.com Inc.	AMZN	18.00
Ameritrade Holding Corp.	AMTD	9.00
CMGI Inc.	CMGI	10.00
CNET Networks, Inc.	CNET	4.00
DoubleClick Inc.	DCLK	4.00
E*Trade Group Inc.	ET	12.00
EarthLink Network, Inc.	ELNK	6.23
eBay Inc.	EBAY	24.00
McAfee Inc.	MFE	7.00
Priceline.com Inc.	PCLN	1.17
RealNetworks, Inc.	RNWK	8.00
Time Warner Inc.	TWX	42.00
Yahoo Inc.	YHOO	52.00

Source: Amex.com

possible to invest in the best sectors, new ETFs make it possible to invest in the hottest commodities and countries, too.

A NEW GOLD INDEX, A NEW CHINA CARD TO PLAY

Wall Street is never slow to bring new products forward when it thinks there's investment demand. It happened with mutual funds and with initial public offerings (IPOs). And now, with much better consequences for investors, it's happening with index funds and ETFs. You're getting more ways to invest in the multiple bull markets springing up in different asset classes and different countries all over the world. I'll give you just two examples here. The industry is growing so quickly that by the time you read this, there will undoubtedly be more. The important thing to see is that your choices are growing. With the right vision and strategy—a subject I'll discuss in Chapter 5—you'll have the perfect tools to profit.

Gold enjoyed one of its strongest bull markets in years in 2004. The ETF industry noticed. First came GLD, or the street TRACKS Gold Shares. This particular vehicle operates as a trust, so it is slightly different from other, similar products. But in principle it is the same as IWM or HHH. Here, GLD allows you to buy something that imitates the performance of the gold price. It's like buying gold without actually buying gold.

Now, there are many people who would tell you that owning some *real* gold is a much better idea than owning *paper* gold, and I'm one of them. But as with all of these ETF strategies, I'm not suggesting that it's all you should do, only that these are strategies you *can* use to complement your other investments and ultimately achieve whatever your investment objectives are.

As I write this, there is talk of a similar investment that allows you to buy crude oil. You can be bullish on crude oil without putting an oil well in your backyard. It won't directly cut down on the cost of filling up your car. But making profits from the rise of crude oil gives you at least some consolation. In Chapter 4, I'll show an ETF that tracks the stocks of major oil companies, rather than the commodity (crude oil) itself. And I'll show you how to turn small price movements in that ETF into large profits.

But you're beginning to see what's going on in the ETF world. Wall Street is creating new indexes and ETFs to track them. Wall Street realizes that if you confine yourself to investing in single stocks, there are many bull markets you'd miss out on. Wall Street, generally, would be fine with this, as long as they were making money. But the proverbial cat is out of the bag, and so now investors are expecting that Wall Street's interests are aligned with the interests of investors like you and me.

That will never entirely be true. But the growth of the ETF industry is making it at least more true. For example, the American Stock Exchange has created a new gold index. It goes by the symbol GDM. There are 36 companies in GDM, including all 12 companies in the Philly Gold Silver Index (XAU) and all 15 companies in the unhedged gold index (HUI). *Why the bigger index?*

In a press release Amex said, "As investors have reawakened to the benefits of investing in gold shares, the gold mining industry has expanded. The new AMEX Gold Miners Index reflects this expansion by combining emerging market producers with established miners to reflect a cross section of the market. With this new comprehensive representation, the AMEX Gold Miners Index may become the new benchmark for the industry."[3]

Because of the overlap in the XAU and HUI, even though there are only 9 more holdings in GDM than the XAU and HUI combined, there are actually 14 new companies included in GDM that are not included on either XAU or HUI. Most of those companies, as you might guess, are not major gold producers but smaller companies (although all the companies in GMD have at least a $100 million market cap and an average daily volume of at least 50,000 shares for the last six months).

What this may mean is a gold index that's actually more responsive to movements in the spot price of gold. That means more volatility—and on the upside, for gold bulls, more leverage (more about leverage in Chapter 4). Think about that for a minute. Here is an index of stocks that may be *more* volatile than the price of gold. That means it could also be an index that moves down more on gold's periodic consolidation moves. That's important for a bull hunter, being able to profit on down moves as well. Remember, we'll take our price moves wherever we can find them and in whichever direction.

Here's the best news. The backers of the index have already said their intent is to create an ETF that tracks the index. You'll be able to buy GDM the same way you can currently buy the Russell 2000 by buying IWM. For investors in commodities, you can expect to see more commodity-based ETFs. Now, instead of using ETFs to buy the best sector, you can use them to buy the best asset class as well. And that's not all.

A BIG RED CHIP AND A BIG RED BUST

It's not just gold that's beginning to benefit from the ETF boom. You can now "buy" China with a single stock. Even better, you can buy options on China, too. In other words, for less than $500, you can buy a call on the fastest-growing economy in the world. Or you can buy a put if you think a hard landing is coming. Amoral, market-neutral traders can (and probably should) do both, starting tomorrow.

The China 25 Index from iShares trades under the symbol FXI. It's made up of 25 of the largest Chinese stocks currently available to international investors. According to a fact sheet:

> The Fund holds H and Red Chip shares of some of the largest liquid Chinese companies. H Shares are securities of companies incorporated in the PRC and nominated by the Chinese government for listing and trading on the Hong Kong Stock Exchange. They're quoted and traded in Hong Kong dollars. . . . Red Chip Shares are securities of Hong Kong incorporated companies that trade on the Hong Kong Stock Exchange. . . . Red Chips are companies that are substantially owned directly or indirectly by the Chinese Government and have the majority of their business interests in Mainland China.[4]

There are some big names in the 25 holdings, including Petrochina, China Mobile, and China Telecom. Nearly 20 percent of the companies in the index are oil and gas outfits. Telecom comes in next at 19 percent, and transportation at 15 percent.

I don't recommend you buy FXI or any Chinese stocks, for that matter. In fact, I think a China bust is in the cards. I'll tell you why I think that in chapters 7 and 8, based on what I saw in China when I visited in the summer of 2004. Besides, I think there are better ways to profit from China's growing economy. I'll tell you about them in Chapter 9, and explain why a bust in Chinese stocks is not necessarily bad news for China's economy.

THE GOOD KIND OF DIVERSIFICATION

The beauty of ETFs is that they let you invest in big-picture trends on three different levels: by sector, by asset class, and by geography.

There are other ways to slice and dice it, of course. But those are the ones that I think will be most useful in the coming years.

There are currently 143 ETFs. Some of them are already valuable tools for investors who know how to use them. For example, you can be long the ETFs in your portfolio and then hedge against that risk with put options on them from time to time. In this strategy, you employ puts to protect against downside movement, a form of insurance that hedges the long position. The ability to use options is also one of the major differences between ETFs and mutual funds and, in the most volatile of conditions, may prove to be one of the more important distinctions.

The ETF industry is in its infancy and the potential strategies for long or short positions, or for protecting long positions with puts, for example, open up whole new realms of investment strategy. Those stockholders who have learned to use listed stock options to create double-digit returns may be among the more successful ETF players in the future because they have already mastered what most consider to be a highly exotic product.

I contend that, to the contrary, options are advantageous vehicles that we can all use to (1) protect existing profits, (2) create additional, potentially handsome short-term income, and (3) hedge existing positions; for example, you can use options to take out paper profits without needing to close long positions.

You can see why ETFs are so attractive. They are flexible and you can employ many more strategies than you ever could with the twentieth-century favorite, mutual funds. You may, in fact, view ETFs as a more flexible evolution beyond the traditional fund, a development well suited to the financial and global realities of the twenty-first century.

More specifically, ETFs—especially combined with strategically selected options—give you more choice for less cost. They're not the right investment for everyone, of course. But given the number of ETF choices now available—many unheard of a decade ago—you should consider them.

You can now be short the bond market, long in small-cap stocks, and both long and short oil at the same time—all with ETFs or options on ETFs. Options on ETFs are exciting for their potential. They are only part of the great changes taking place in the world's markets. These moves are being led by some powerful economic themes that shape our investment outlook. I'll talk about that outlook—especially the rising powers of India and China—in Chapter 4. But let's take a brief, bull-hunting look at using options on ETFs.

THINKING THE UNTHINKABLE: ETF OPTIONS STRATEGIES FOR A DANGEROUS WORLD

> We have a strategy drawn up for the destruction of Anglo-Saxon civiliza-
> tion and for the uprooting of the Americans and the English.
> **—Hassan Abassi, Iranian Revolutionary Guards Intelligence Theoretician[1]**

What better way to celebrate your arrival in Paris than with a bottle of wine? This was my plan when I first arrived in the city in the late afternoon in October 2002. I'd just arrived after an eight-hour, overnight flight from Baltimore and hauled all my bags into a tiny third-floor rented apartment on the Rue Etienne Marcel in the second arrondissement.

On the ground floor of the building next door is a wine shop run by a middle-aged man named Claude who has long white hair and loves American jazz. He tells me his daughter once dated the bass player in Metallica. Small world.

Claude sold me quite a few bottles of wine over the next year and a half. I learned a little about jazz and a lot more about wine. But on that first night, with my first bottle of Côtes du Rhône, I learned an important and unexpected lesson about investing: You cannot open a bottle of wine with an eggbeater.

It is one thing to have a set of tools at your disposal. It is quite another to know how, where, and when to use them. Chapter 3 showed that index funds and exchange-traded funds give you a whole new world of investment choices that most investors have never enjoyed. You can turn events that are largely out of your control into opportunities. This chapter will show you how to turn some of the world's most potent dangers into even more potent opportunities. But first, one more important note on the French.

MAKE YOURSELF UNCOMFORTABLE

My apartment in Paris was fully furnished, except for a corkscrew. My French colleagues later told me the absence of the corkscrew was a gross oversight by the landlady. They were embarrassed for me, and for all of la France, which provides a level of comfortable living that appears effortless. It isn't, of course. There is a hidden cost to everything. But we'll get to that in Chapter 5. Contrary to what you see in the press, though, the average Frenchman or woman is not that different from you, except, perhaps, at the dinner table.

The French take their food seriously. A cup of coffee or a three-hour dinner is not just about the quality of the food or the wine (I never eat the cheese; it's bad for my stomach). Eating is a social experience in France. What's more, serving food is a serious profession for which men and women go to school in France. That may seem silly to Americans. But you can see why a Frenchman who deals with food professionally chafes at being bossed around by Americans who deal with food recreationally. For the French, food is serious pleasure, to be relished and treated with respect. For Americans, food is serious business, to be consumed and treated with salt.

Americans want prompt service, healthy portions, and plenty of attention for an extra fork, some more napkins, or another Coke. The French want to be left alone to eat, talk, and digest. I am convinced that much of the animosity between America and France stems from the difference in the way we treat food. A lot would be resolved if both nations treated food the way the English do, namely as something to be deep-fried, eaten, and tolerated between cups of coffee or pints of lager.

This culinary side trip has served a purpose, I hope. When you visit foreign countries, it takes you out of your comfort zone. Other people have different customs. The food is different. Often the language is different.

Making yourself uncomfortable causes you to see things you wouldn't otherwise see. It changes your perspective. It's also a way of showing yourself that what once seemed too challenging to attempt is actually not as hard as it looks. But what does it mean to make yourself uncomfortable as investors? There are three answers to this question.

First, it means being bold enough to think unconventionally. This, of course, is the whole bull hunter philosophy. You recognize that the world is always changing and that what worked yesterday may not work tomorrow. You are willing to try new approaches to achieve your investment goals.

Second, it means using all the tools at your disposal. This can sometimes be even more difficult than allowing yourself to think differently. Most of us are lazy. We'd do as little as possible to achieve our investment goals, if we could get away with it. But these days, doing as little as possible is the same thing as doing nothing at all. What I hope to have shown you in Chapter 3, and what I hope to show you in this one, is that using new tools doesn't have to be intimidating. Uncomfortable, yes—probably the way my mom felt when she got her first VCR in the mid-1980s. For her, setting the clock on the VCR was like landing a 747 on an aircraft carrier. But after the first few times, we find that most challenges we feared aren't nearly as difficult as we imagined.

Finally, you have to be willing to ask the questions no one else wants to ask. In the investment world, thinking about the future can be a dangerous game. You can't predict the future. If you invest your money based on faulty predictions, you could easily lose it. Yet the investor's greatest challenge is to figure out what price to pay today for future earnings that are unpredictable. The further you go into the future, the harder it is to tell what tomorrow will bring and what you should be willing to pay for it today. That's why buying stocks at a high price-to-earnings multiple is a large, and almost always foolish, gamble on the future. You are betting that 20 or 30 years from now, business will be just as good and even better for the company you're buying today at a high price.

But the stock market looks ahead, not behind. And so we have to look ahead, too, to try to see what's coming, if not in the earnings picture, then at least in the bigger picture. You're going to be investing in a stock market driven by geopolitical events as much as earnings, probably for the rest of your investment life. That means trying to decipher what events like war in the Middle East or high personal debt levels in America might mean for the stock market.

It's not an exact science. In the next three chapters, I'm going to show you what I think are the large themes that are moving global markets and how to invest in them conservatively. In this chapter, I'm going to show you that it's also possible to look into the future and make some intelligent speculations on what *might* happen. Using options on index funds and exchange-traded funds is one way that modern investors can insure themselves against large, macroeconomic risks. It is not foolproof insurance. And it is not without risk. But in a dangerous and uncomfortable world, it is one practical way to begin putting the tools at your disposal to work.

While the events I'm about to show you may not happen (or may have *already* happened by the time you read this), it's also important to remember that event-driven market moves are taking place all the time and all over the globe. What follows are examples of how to turn those events into opportunities for profit. Rest assured that long after the geopolitical and economic events I tell you about here have resolved themselves, others will have sprung up to replace them and to offer you new opportunity.

$100 OIL AND THE STRAIT OF HORMUZ

In a speech I gave in Chicago in 2004, I made the case for $100-a-barrel oil to 150 options investors. They were shocked, skeptical, and intrigued, by turns. I told them what I'll tell you now. Event-driven investment moves—the kind where an external event shocks markets and causes a big move up or down in a sector or the whole market—are nearly impossible to predict. But strategic foresight can help you prepare for some of them.

One of the largest geopolitical events looming on the horizon today is a potential conflict with Iran. Iran is a charter member of President George W. Bush's Axis of Evil. Iran is near the top of the president's foreign policy agenda for his second term.

At stake is whether Iran will become a nuclear power. It's not clear how this would change the world. In any event, it's a discussion beyond the scope of this book. What *is* clear is that the mullahs who run Iran, judging by the quote I placed at the beginning of this chapter, have a strategic vision of their own. To investors, what ought to be even clearer is what the consequences of a war with Iran would mean: $100 oil.

Any economist worth his or her pocket protector will tell you that $100 oil is not economically sustainable. The world simply could not afford to pay $100 for a barrel of oil—for a sustained period of time. It would create a world of oil haves and have-nots, and might even precipitate oil wars between nations desperately competing over a scarce and expensive natural resource. Not only would it drive U.S. gasoline prices to unimaginable heights, the shock of such a dramatic rise in energy costs would throw the world's economy into a deep and painful recession, if not a depression. But that doesn't mean it couldn't happen anyway—at least for a few days or weeks.

The map in Figure 4.1 shows the very narrow strait of Hormuz, through which nearly 85 percent of the oil from the Persian Gulf passes, on its way to Japan, Western Europe, and North America. You can see quite clearly that Iran dominates that strait to the northern and eastern sides.

You don't have to be Dr. Strangelove to envision what the Iranian strategy might be against the U.S. economy. I say *economy* and not *military*. The nature of an Iranian counterattack would mostly likely be to strike against U.S. economic interests. And what greater interest than oil? After all, it's much easier to drive the price of oil to $100 a barrel and instigate a political firestorm in Washington, D.C., than it is to defend against American strategic bombers and precision-guided

FIGURE 4.1 An energy chokepoint, a geopolitical
flashpoint: the Strait of Hormuz.
(Source: Energy Information Administration)

munitions. Iran knows that America and all of Europe and Japan are
addicted to oil.

It is obvious from Figure 4.1 and Figures 4.2A, B, and C that
much of that oil comes from the Persian Gulf and must physically
pass through the Strait of Hormuz to get to its final destinations. By
choking off the supply of oil at this strategic point, Iran could exert
enormous pressure on the United States, which would itself be pres-
sured by those who desperately count on Middle East oil and want
no part of America's quarrel with Iran.

With such a potentially high economic price to pay for a war with
Iran, I've been told by some strategic investors that the United States
would never risk it. But here is a question to make you uncomfortable: If it is plain for all to see that the way to America's weakness is
through interrupting the flow of oil from the Persian Gulf, isn't it just

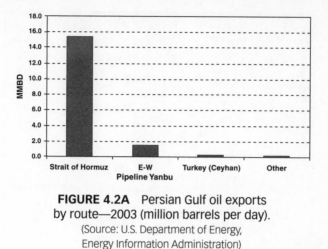

FIGURE 4.2A Persian Gulf oil exports by route—2003 (million barrels per day).
(Source: U.S. Department of Energy, Energy Information Administration)

a matter of time until someone tries it? Instead of fighting a war conventionally, why not try economic warfare, attacking what makes a country strong to begin with—its economy? In total economic warfare, you attack a country's access to natural resources or its currency. By attacking its economy, you indirectly weaken its ability to attack you militarily.

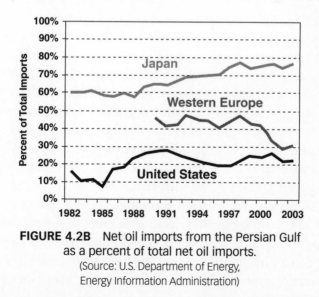

FIGURE 4.2B Net oil imports from the Persian Gulf as a percent of total net oil imports.
(Source: U.S. Department of Energy, Energy Information Administration)

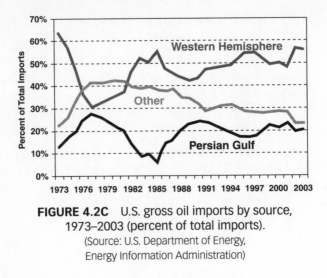

FIGURE 4.2C U.S. gross oil imports by source,
1973–2003 (percent of total imports).
(Source: U.S. Department of Energy,
Energy Information Administration)

FINANCIAL TERRORISM AND AN ENERGY PEARL HARBOR

If not Iran, then perhaps al Qaeda? And if not at the Strait of Hormuz, then perhaps at the Saudi oil refinery of Ras Tanura, one of the world's biggest and most productive? Even the British Broadcasting Corporation (BBC) sees what could happen. In 2004, the BBC aired a docudrama about what's been called an "energy Pearl Harbor."

Here's how it works (in the mind of the BBC). A rogue Middle Eastern oil trader works for a major money-center bank. Working in concert with his terrorist conspirators in Saudi Arabia, the trader takes an enormous leveraged position short crude oil, much as a hedge fund or institution might. At the same time, al Qaeda terrorists target the Saudi oil facility of Ras Tanura, the largest oil complex in the world. Ras Tanura cranks out almost 4.5 million barrels per day. Former CIA agent Robert Baer wrote in his book *Sleeping With the Devil* (Crown, 2003) that an attack like the one on the U.S.S. *Cole* in 2000 could knock out Ras Tanura for weeks. Baer also speculates that if the oil processing facility of Abqaiq were attacked via a hijacked jetliner, it would reduce Saudi production by as much as 4 million barrels per day for up to seven months.

You get the picture. The trader takes a huge position short. The oil price spikes on the terror attack. The leveraged short position becomes a form of financial terrorism. The banks' losses mount to the stratosphere. They hit their capital reserve requirements. They must liquidate others' assets. They are forced to sell, causing a wave of selling by other financial institutions.

The BBC presentation of the story morphed into the trader's "real" motives. He was upset with his bosses' focus on profits and turned out *not* to be in collaboration with al Qaeda. It's all fiction anyway. But if you were looking for a way to put Western economies in checkmate, sending the oil price sky-high and precipitating a financial crisis at the same time, it's hard to think of a better way—if you practiced total economic warfare, that is.

OPTIONS ON THE PRICE SPIKE

Whether any of the scenarios I outlined ever happen doesn't really matter. There are two things that do. One, events like this can and do have real effects on asset prices. Two, you can take real investment steps to profit from them, even if you can't prevent them, and hope they never happen. But how? First you'd have to find out what to buy. Then you'd have to find out when to buy it and for how much.

In the preceding example, what you'd look for is an index or exchange-traded fund that imitates the price of crude oil. If you're expecting the price of crude oil to rise on a dramatic interruption in supply, you want a proxy for crude oil that moves with the oil price. Not only that, you'd want an index or an ETF you could buy options on—in this case a *call* option.

More on options later. And at the end of this chapter you'll find an up-to-date list of exchange-traded funds and indexes on which you can trade options. It's growing every day. But in the current world of index and exchange-traded funds, you have at least six different oil-related ETFs that are optionable:

1. XLE—Energy Select Sector SPDR
2. IYE—iShares Trust—DJ U.S. Energy Sector Index Fund
3. OIX—CBOE Oil Index Options

4. MGO—Morgan Stanley Oil Services Options

5. OSX—Oil Service Sector

6. OIH—Oil Services HOLDRs Trust

As I mentioned in Chapter 3, you can find out just which companies are basketed or indexed in each of these. Some focus on major, diversified companies like ExxonMobil, ChevronTexaco, and BP. Others are composed of smaller oil service companies that sell the parts and equipment to make oil fields all over the world productive.

Of these choices, there's one in particular that mimics the price of crude oil. That makes it a good proxy. Instead of trading a crude oil futures contract, you can simply buy a call option on an ETF. But before I explain which of these I like the most, let me give you a brief description of what options are and how they work.

OPTIONS, THE BRIEFER COURSE

This is a fast review of options basics. There are plenty of good books that go into greater detail. *Getting Started in Options,* by Michael C. Thomsett (John Wiley, 2005); *Options Made Easy,* by Guy Cohen (Financial Times/Prentice Hall, 2002); and *McMillan on Options,* by Lawrence G. McMillan (John Wiley, 1996). But before jumping into specific options strategies, you need to make sure that you appreciate the risks involved.

There are two kinds of options: calls and puts. A *call* gives the buyer the right (but not the obligation) to purchase shares of an underlying security (such as an ETF). The option fixes the price, so the buyer would exercise that option only if the market price were higher than the fixed *strike price* of the option. As a call buyer, you hope the market value rises. The opposite is true for call sellers. A seller gives up the contractual rights to someone else and, if the call is exercised, the seller has to deliver the specified number of shares in the underlying security, at the fixed price.

A *put* is the opposite of a call. A put buyer acquires the right (but not the obligation) to *sell* shares of an underlying security, at a fixed strike price, at any time before expiration. So if a buyer is holding a put and the price falls, shares can be sold at a fixed price higher than current market value. A put *seller* hopes that share value will not fall below the strike price; if value does fall, the seller is required to buy shares of the underlying security at the fixed strike price.

To complicate the risk/reward scenario a little more, consider this: Option buyers have to pay to purchase their options, but option sellers receive money when they open positions. The exact degree of risk depends on whether a seller has shares or not, or in the case of puts, whether the seller would be willing to pick up shares above current market value.

Those are the basic rules for options, but completely understanding the risks requires more careful study. Options are interesting because their risks range from highly speculative to very conservative, all depending on how you position yourself. The terminology, trading rules, and risks make options exciting and interesting, but dangerous as well. The key to options plays is that they are exceptional ways to leverage your money—to control a large amount of equity for relatively small capital at risk.

With options on ETFs, you capitalize on global trends like rising oil prices with the possibility of bigger gains with fixed risk and a cost of usually less than $1,000 per contract. Let me give you a specific example.

Figure 4.3 shows the price movement of OIH, the Oil Service HOLDRs. You can see I've indicated two separate "trades" on OIH: once when I recommended to my readers that they buy puts, and once when I recommended that they buy calls. Both trades profited.

Bullish Oil with OIH	*Bearish Oil with OIH*
OIH Oct 70 calls	OIH Nov 80 puts
Bought 8/24/04 for	Bought 10/25/04
$2.50/contract	for $1.30/contract
Sold 9/7/04 for	Sold on 10/28 for
$6.40/contract	$2.40/contract
7% move in OIH	3.75% move in OIH
Option gained 156%	Option gained 84%

OIH Daily ━

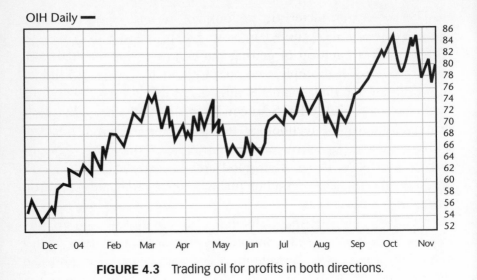

FIGURE 4.3   Trading oil for profits in both directions.

The fact that the options gained so much while the up and down moves in the underlying index were so comparatively small is what traders call *leverage*. It's why investors like trading options. You can turn a small move in an underlying stock or ETF into a large gain. Imagine the effect a large move in OIH might have on its options.

Why did I pick OIH? First, as I said, it correlated to the price movements in crude oil. There's no point in buying something as a proxy if it doesn't track what you're trying to track. But there are characteristics you should look for when choosing an ETF or index to trade options.

The first is liquidity. This means being able to buy and sell easily because there are lots of other traders to buy and sell to. For the big index options like the triple Qs, the Dow Diamonds (DIA), or the S&P SPDRs (SPY), this isn't a problem. In fact, trading volumes for the triple Qs are usually much larger than for any single stock listed on the Nasdaq. That's an indication of the appeal of ETFs and index funds. They make it easy to buy a sector, asset, or country in just one stock. But make sure to note the trading volumes if you're thinking of entering the options market. With so many new products coming onto the market, not all of them will attract the same amount of capital. Some will be illiquid. Avoid those.

The second characteristic to look for is small spreads on the options prices you're quoted by your broker or an online service. This is really a question of getting the best price for the trade you want to make. For example, two popular ways to trade semiconductor stocks are the Philadelphia Semiconductor Index (SOX) and the Semiconductor HOLDRs. Semiconductors are often thought of as a leading indicator of technology stocks because all electronic and computer goods need semiconductors of some sort. When semiconductor demand is strong, it's a good sign for tech stocks. When it's weak, watch out below (and buy puts on HHH!). Which would you trade options on?

As Figure 4.4 shows, the difference in performance is virtually indistinguishable—as well it should be. The SOX is made up of 19 companies while SMH is made up of 20, and they are computed in different ways. This explains why SMH slightly underperformed in 2004. It is not actively managed, the way a mutual fund is. But an index, like the SOX, is completely passive, being rebalanced once a year on average. SMH's fees and expenses may also account for a slight underperformance.

But if the performance is basically the same, you can see that the

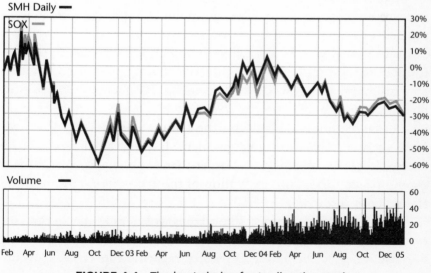

FIGURE 4.4 The best choice for trading the semis.

volume on SMH has grown enormously in the last year. SOX is an index, and you can trade options on it. But SMH is a stock that investors can be long or short in their portfolio. As a result, it has become a more popular—and much more liquid—way to buy and sell semiconductors in a basket. Average daily volume is around 24 million shares.

With more volume, the spreads tend to be smaller on puts and calls. This is not always the case, however. Options pricing itself is an entirely different discipline. It is a difficult subject because there are lots of variables—the main ones being time, intrinsic value, and something mathematicians call *delta*.

I will leave a longer discussion of options pricing for another book. For now, the main point to keep in mind is that if you get the right price and trade a liquid ETF or index, it *is* possible to turn major geopolitical events into occasions for profit. In fact, I manage and oversee a service that does just that for subscribers to *Strategic Options Alert*.

It is not, as I said, an exact science. It all starts with making an observation about the world and then asking yourself what is the best way to profit. Some traders prefer black boxes and systems that automatically do their thinking for them. This works for some of them. It does not work for me.

I think the world is too large and too full of opportunities to limit yourself to black boxes and systems. Yes, you need to be disciplined. Most investors lose money trading options. They have no clear strategy and no clear trading philosophy. But if you have both, then your only real limits are the scope of your trading ideas and the size of your bank account.

You should not trade options if it's money you can't afford to lose. They are risky. But used intelligently, they can also help you reduce the risk in your core portfolio. Used with precision and good timing, they can even turn major geopolitical and economic events into surprising opportunities.

You could trade options on OIH, buying long-dated calls for example, to hedge your risk against an oil war in the Gulf. Will it stop the war? No. Will it keep you from paying higher prices at the pump? No. Can you make money when oil prices rise by owing calls on an oil ETF that tracks crude oil prices? Absolutely.

You can also use SMH to anticipate what's going on in the tech sector. A downtrend in SMH might be your signal to buy puts on HHH or some other technology/Internet proxy. Or a sudden up-trend might tell you it's time to buy calls.

With options on ETFs and indexes, you can be both bullish and bearish, depending on price movements. That's exactly what a bull hunter should be. You're not concerned with where things *should* be going. You're concerned with how to profit, regardless of their direction.

That's not to say, however, that what *ought* to happen in the markets doesn't happen. To show you what I mean, and to give you one final example of trading options on ETFs and index funds, let's look at that the black plague on the American economy: consumer debt.

SHORT THE AMERICAN CONSUMER IN ONE STOCK

In an airport waiting lounge on my way back to London from a speech in Chicago, I noticed the money section of *USA Today* lying under a discarded bag of potato chips. What jumped out at me were these figures:

- $84,454 in average household personal debt in America
- $473,456—your share of the Social Security and Medicare bill
- $53 trillion in federal debt and unfunded liabilities

You have probably seen and heard as much about America's debt problems as I have. In fact, so much has been written about the debt that I wonder if we're not immune to it by now. Spending more than we can afford has become a habit for most of us. It doesn't seem unusual. And it certainly doesn't seem immoral. But it is.

Passing on burdens to our children and grandchildren so that we can have everything we want today is a giant national failing of character. I say that as a man without any children of my own. But I have

10 nieces and nephews and I'm now a godfather. We owe it to these kids to get our private fiscal houses in order. We also owe it to them to get our public finances in order. Most of all, we ought to realize that we have other obligations in the world than making ourselves happy and "living for today." I will step off my soapbox now and return to the subject at hand with a question: *It's immoral and unethical to raid your children's financial future for your own personal pleasure. But is the creation of all that debt a tradable event?*

Remember, part of being a bull hunter is asking unseemly questions. Or, to put it another way, what someone else might consider an unseemly question is usually a problem that can be turned into a solution, if you get beyond the fear of asking it. Your alternative is to ask no hard questions and then be surprised when events beyond your control begin to destroy your carefully ignored financial plans.

But if you're willing to look at an unpleasant reality for what it is, you're one step closer to robbing it of its ability to, well, rob you. It's much better to confront a financial fear than pretend that it does not exist. Then you can decide which tool you want to use in order to turn the crisis into an opportunity.

THE DEBT THREAT

The Cambridge Credit Counseling Corp. reports that the average American household has $14,000 in credit card debt. That's in addition to the mortgage debt and auto loan debt I mentioned earlier. Many commentators say that because debt service payments are only about 14 percent of disposable income—high, but not crushingly so—consumer debt is no problem. Incomes are rising, so the theory goes, so the debt is "serviceable," meaning monthly interest and mortgage payments are not overly burdensome.

In Chapter 5 I'll show you one of the unintended consequences of globalization. It has actually lowered average American wages. The bad news is that it will continue to do so for most Americans. The worse news is that as incomes fall or grow more slowly than debt, the debt will get harder and harder to pay off in the long term.

You wonder how many people are thinking about the longer term, though. And I don't mean next week or next year. Rather, the year after that, and 10 years after that, when the baby boomers hope to retire en masse. "The big picture is that we're a debtor nation but remain the most profligate spenders," writes Howard David-owitz, president of Davidowitz & Associates, in a CNN/Money article.[2] Davidowitz looks at the personal balance sheet and shudders: ". . . we're borrowing our brains out. The most concerning thing is the level of savings is at less than 1% of personal income. I look at mortgage refinancing activity declining because of rising interest rates. I look at a sluggish job market and these big credit spending levels. To me it shows that consumer spending levels will not be sustainable."

This long and historic falling savings rates (see Figure 4.5)—coupled with a long and historic rise in debt levels, is a good reason to be suspicious of America's retail sales industry. Now, it's true that many an analyst has forecast the demise of American consumers and their profligate habits. I now add myself to that illustrious list.

Actually, I've been on the list for at least five years now. I write it virtually every month to my *Strategic Investment* subscribers. When I give a speech, I remind whomever will listen that it's hard to get rich

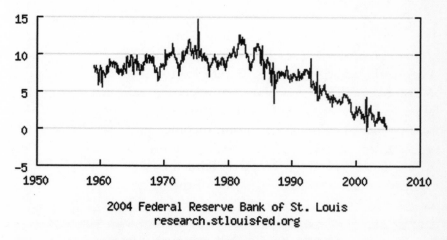

2004 Federal Reserve Bank of St. Louis
research.stlouisfed.org

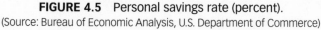

FIGURE 4.5 Personal savings rate (percent).
(Source: Bureau of Economic Analysis, U.S. Department of Commerce)

when you spend more than you earn. Lately, I have also been telling them to consider buying put options on a basket of retail stocks that trades under they symbol RTH.

Figure 4.6 yields at least two pieces of investment intelligence. First, you can see that, like SMH, the trading volume on RTH took off in 2004. This again shows that ETFs and index funds and baskets of stocks—anything that makes it easier for you to invest in large themes quickly and easily—are gaining in popularity. Liquidity is growing and spreads are dropping. From a trading standpoint, the chart also tells me that it's going to take an unexpected revival in the American economy for RTH to make a new high at about 100. When you find out what RTH is made up of, you'll see why.

RTH is a basket of 20 retail stocks, including Amazon.com, Wal-Mart, Home Depot, and Walgreen (see Table 4.1). Here's the trading proposition before you as a bull hunter: If you believe American consumers are in great shape, that the American labor market will produce more jobs and higher wages in the next five years, that there is a pent-up demand for consumption in America, that low interest

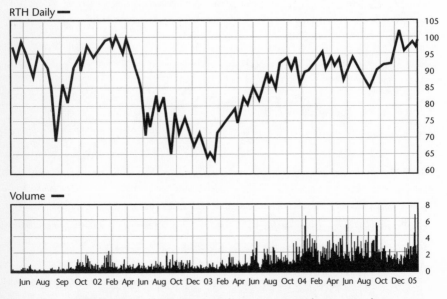

FIGURE 4.6 Short the American consumer in one stock.

TABLE 4.1 AMERICA'S 20 BIGGEST RETAILERS

Stock	Ticker
Albertsons Inc.	ABS
Amazon.com Inc.	AMZN
Best Buy Co. Inc.	BBY
Costco Wholesale Corp.	COST
CVS Corp.	CVS
Federated Department Stores	FD
GAP Inc.	GPS
Home Depot Inc.	HD
Kroger Co.	KR
Kohl's Corp.	KSS
Limited Brands, Inc.	LTD
Lowe's Companies	LOW
May Department Stores Co.	MAY
RadioShack Corp.	RSH
Safeway Inc.	SWY
Sears, Roebuck and Co.	S
Target Corp.	TGT
TJX Companies Inc.	TJX
Walgreen Co.	WAG
Wal-Mart Stores	WMT

Source: Amex.com

rates and easy credit are here to stay, and that the debt isn't a drag on future purchases, you'd buy calls on RTH.

But if you think the opposite is true—that the coming years will see consumers rein in their spending or go bankrupt—you'll buy puts. You could also buy puts, by the way, if you are long one of the stocks in the index and want to hedge that risk with an options position. It's not a perfect hedge, of course. You might still lose money on your long or any stock you were trying to hedge against.

But the beauty of index and exchange-traded fund options is that your risk is fixed. It's simply the cost of the options contract and the number of contracts *you* choose to buy. Can you still lose money? Of course. But the risk is controlled. And if you're right about the big underlying trend, the leverage you get with options can make it worth your while.

Retail stocks are also headed for a rocky future because the baby boomers are retiring *and* have a lot of debt. Recent numbers from the Federal Reserve's Survey of Consumers show that 24.7 percent of households headed by someone age 65 to 74 had mortgage debt in 1995. That number grew to 32 percent in 2001. The boomers are actually adding debt as they get older. Old habits die hard. Bad habits die not at all.

GLOBAL VILLAGE, SAME NATURE

If you think I'm being harder on Americans than they deserve, I'm not. Americans are not any better or any worse than other people, we just have more credit cards. The truth is, in the parts of the world that I've been lucky enough to see so far, I've found that most people are the same. People work, marry, raise children, try to put food on the table. We get old and then we die.

In between, we struggle. We try to survive the snares and obstacles set in our paths by governments. Occasionally we succeed, sometimes by luck and sometimes by design.

In some places, the struggles are far greater. There's a difference in kind between not having cable TV and not having suitable drinking water. It's a safe bet that the average American or Western European has a higher standard of living today than 99 percent of all the people who have ever lived on this planet—and that's *with* all the dangers we face.

Life is generally good for most of us in the West. At the very least, it's far more comfortable than most places on the planet. But how long will our comfortable, credit-driven, cheeseburger paradise last? To answer that, we'll have to take a step back from the world of precision-guided investments and the options market and look at a much bigger, strategic picture.

But before then, take a look at this partial list of ETF, index, and interest rate options. The list of new products—and solutions to investment problems—grows each month.

ETF, Index, and Interest Rate Options

iShares from Barclays

AGG—Options on iShares® Lehman Aggregate Bond Fund

DGT—streetTRACKS®—DJ Global Titans Index Fund

DIA—Options on DIA-MONDS®

DVY—iShares DJ Select Dividend

EFA—Options on iShares MSCI EAFE® Exchange-Traded Fund

IBB—iShares® Nasdaq® Biotechnology

IDU—iShares DJ® U.S. Utilities Sector

IEF—iShares Lehman 7–10 Year Treasury Bond Fund

IGM—iShares Goldman Sachs® Technology Index

IGN—iShares® Goldman Sachs Networking Index Fund

IGV—iShares Goldman Sachs Software Index Fund

IGW—iShares Goldman Sachs Semiconductor Index Fund

IWB—iShares Russell 1000® Index Fund

IWD—iShares Russell 1000 Value Index Fund

IWF—iShares Russell 1000 Growth Index Fund

IWM—iShares Russell 2000® Index Fund

IWN—iShares Russell 2000 Value Index Fund

IWO—iShares Russell 2000 Growth Index Fund

IWP—iShares Russell Midcap® Growth Index Fund

IWR—iShares Russell Midcap Index Fund

IWS—iShares Russell Midcap Value Index Fund

IWV—iShares Russell 3000® Index Fund

IWW—iShares Russell 3000 Value Index Fund

IWZ—iShares Russell 3000 Growth Index Fund

IYE—iShares Trust—DJ U.S. Energy Sector Index Fund

IYH—iShares Trust—DJ U.S. Healthcare Sector Index Fund

IYY—iShares DJ U.S. Total Market

LQD—iShares GS$ InvesTop Corporate Bond Fund

OEF—Options on iShares® S&P 100® Index Fund

ONQ—Options on Fidelity® Nasdaq Composite Index® Tracking Stock

QQQ—Nasdaq 100® Index Tracking Stocks

SHY—iShares Lehman 1–3 Year Treasury Bond Fund

TLT—iShares Lehman 20+ Year Treasury Bond Fund

SPY—SPDR® Options

XLB—Materials Select Sector SPDR

XLE—Energy Select Sector SPDR

XLF—Financial Select Sector SPDR

XLI—Industrial Select Sector SPDR

XLK—Technology Select Sector SPDR

XLP—Consumer Staples Select Sector SPDR

XLU—Utilities Select Sector SPDR

XLV—Health Care Select Sector SPDR

XLY—Consumer Discretionary Select Sector SPDR

HOLDRs from Merrill Lynch

BBH—Biotech HOLDRs Trust

BDH—Broadband HOLDRs Trust

HHH—Internet HOLDRs Trust

IAH—Internet Architect HOLDRs Trust

OIH—Oil Services HOLDRs Trust

PPH—Pharmaceutical HOLDRs Trust

RKH—Regional Bank HOLDRs Trust

RTH—Retail HOLDRs Trust

SMH—Semiconductor HOLDRs Trust

SWH—Software HOLDRs Trust

TBH—Telebras HOLDRs Trust

TTH—Telecom HOLDRs Trust

UTH—Utilities HOLDRs Trust

WMH—Wireless HOLDRs Trust

Chicago Board Options Exchange (CBOE) Listings

DJX—Dow Jones Industrial Average

Dow Jones Industrial Average LEAPS

OEX®—S&P 100® Index Options—American

OEX®—S&P 100® Index LEAPS—American

XEO®—European-Style S&P 100® Index Options

XEO®—European-Style S&P 100® LEAPS

SPX—S&P 500® Index Options

SPX—(Reduced-Value) LEAPS

SPL—S&P Long-Dated Options

SML—S&P® Small-Cap 600 Index Options

NDX—Nasdaq 100® Index Options

MNXSM—CBOE Mini-NDX Index Options

MML—CBOE Mini-NDX Long-Dated Options

GTC—GSTI™ Composite Index Options

RUI—Russell 1000® Index

RLG—Russell 1000® Growth Index

RLV—Russell 1000® Value Index

RUT—Russell 2000® Index

RMN—Mini-Russell 2000® Index Options

RUO—Russell 2000® Growth Index

RUJ—Russell 2000® Value Index

RUA—Russell 3000® Index

RAG—Russell 3000® Growth Index

RAV—Russell 3000® Value Index

RMC—Russell Midcap® Index

RDG—Russell Midcap® Growth Index

RMV—Russell Midcap® Value Index

NFT—Morgan Stanley Multinational Company Index

Dow Jones Index Options

DJX—Dow Jones Industrial Average

Dow Jones Industrial Average LEAPS

DTX—Dow Jones Transportation Average

Dow Jones Transportation Average LEAPS

DUX—Dow Jones Utility Average

DJR—Dow Jones Equity REIT Index

MUT—Dow 10 Index

ECM—Dow Jones Internet Commerce Index

Nasdaq Index Options

NDX—Nasdaq 100® Index Options

MNXSM—CBOE Mini-NDX Index Options

MML—CBOE Mini-NDX Long-Dated Options

Russell Index Options

RUI—Russell 1000® Index

RLG—Russell 1000® Growth Index

RLV—Russell 1000® Value Index

RUT—Russell 2000® Index

RMN—Mini-Russell 2000® Index

RUO—Russell 2000® Growth Index

RUJ—Russell 2000® Value Index

RUA—Russell 3000® Index

RAG—Russell 3000® Growth Index

RAV—Russell 3000® Value Index

RMC—Russell Midcap® Index

RDG—Russell Midcap® Growth Index

RMV—Russell Midcap® Value Index

CBOE Sector Index Options

GOX—CBOE Gold Index Options

INX—CBOE Internet Index Options

OIX—CBOE Oil Index Options

TXX—CBOE Technology Index

Goldman Sachs Technology Index Options

GHA—GSTI™ Hardware Index Options

GIN—GSTI™ Internet Index Options

GIP—GSTI™ Multimedia Networking Index Options

GSM—GSTI™ Semiconductor Index Options

GSO—GSTI™ Software Index Options

GSV—GSTI™ Services Index Options

GTC—GSTI™ Composite Index Options

Morgan Stanley Index Options

MVR—Morgan Stanley Retail Index Options

MVB—Morgan Stanley Biotech Index Options

MGO—Morgan Stanley Oil Services Options

NFT—Morgan Stanley Multinational Company Index

International Index Options

CYX—CBOE China Index Options

EYR—CBOE Asia 25 Index Options

EOR—CBOE Euro 25 Index Options

MEX—CBOE Mexico Index Options

NFT—Morgan Stanley Multinational Company Index

Philadelphia Exchange Sector Index Options

BKX—Bank Index

KSX—Capital Markets Index

KIX—Insurance Index

BMX—Computer Box Maker Sector

DFX—Defense Sector

RXS—Drug Sector

XEX—Europe Sector

XAU—Gold/Silver Sector

HGX—Housing Sector

OSX—Oil Service Sector

SOX—Semiconductor Sector

UTY—Utility Sector

SCQ—Cable, Media & Entertainment Index

SGV—Casino Gaming Index

ESU—Education Index

FSQ—Footware & Athletic Index

SMQ—Investment Managers Index

DSQ—Restaurant Index

SEZ—Semiconductor Capital Equipment Index

SDL—Semiconductor Device Index

RSQ—Specialty Retail Index

STQ—Steel Producers Index

DOT—TheStreet.com Internet Sector

Interest Rate Options Product Specifications

IRX—13-Week Treasury Bill

FVX—5-Year Treasury Note

TNX—10-Year Treasury Note

TYX—30-Year Treasury Bond

CHAPTER 5

THE MONEY MIGRATION

Everything that rises goes rightly to its ruin.

—**Mephistopheles, in Goethe's** *Faust*

"Dan, when are you going to India?" Bill Bonner asked me in September of 2003.

"Hmm. How about next June?" I said.

"Sounds good. Let me know what you find out."

That's how it started. It began with a comment and progressed to a three-month trip to parts east. It continues in this book, and hopefully beyond. But in our remaining chapters together, I'll tell you about where I went, what I saw, and what the best investment opportunities are for the next 10 years. I'll also tell you where to eat barbecue crickets in Japan, deep-fried prawns in Perth, and the best Peking duck in China.

Before I was done with my Journey to the East, I visited 11 countries over six months. I made stops in Dallas, Denver, New Orleans, Chicago, Vancouver, Puerto Vallarta, Tokyo, Hong Kong, Shanghai,

Nanjing, Beijing, Bombay, Bangkok, Koh Samui, Perth, Sydney, San Diego, New York, Paris, London, Washington, D.C., Baltimore, Venice, and Estes Park, Colorado.

Don't get me wrong. I'm no Jim Rogers. A few days or a week in a major city staying in a downtown hotel does not qualify you to make penetrating observations about the character of a nation and its future economic prospects. To do that you'd have to do what Jim Rogers has done twice: find out what countries are like from the people who really know how things work—the border guards, prostitutes, businesspeople, and bartenders.

THE DAY AFTER RECKONING DAY

My goal was more modest: figure out what happens the day after reckoning day. The year I arrived in Paris to work with publisher Bill Bonner and my friend Addison Wiggin, they were working on a book of their own. It was called *Financial Reckoning Day* (John Wiley, 2003). At first, they wouldn't, or couldn't, say what the book was about, only that they were trying to show how the investment world had gone completely mad, and what the likely consequences would be—a "soft, slow-motion depression," as it turned out.

As I talked to them about their book, I continued to write to my own readers at *Strategic Investment* about how to navigate increasingly dangerous U.S. markets. It also became obvious that there were two parts to the story unfolding in the world's economy. The first part was about the destruction of wealth that comes with a great financial bust. Bill and Addison's book is the history of how we got here and how it all might end. *Financial Reckoning Day* is about the end of American economic supremacy.

But the sun will come up, even after a financial judgment day. The important question now is, what kind of world will it shine down on? If America's economic fortunes are waning, whose are waxing?

The economist Joseph Schumpeter coined the now famous phrase "creative destruction." Schumpeter explained that economic growth is a dynamic, organic, and evolutionary process. Old, tired, slow, and unwieldy businesses (and economies) get destroyed by young, fast, energetic, and smaller firms (or economies) that tend to give consumers new products, better choices, and lower prices.

You see creative destruction at work everywhere you look around the world. Some people call it globalization. I call it the *money migration*. In simple terms, it means that money (capital) will always migrate to where the returns are highest. When it migrates, it brings investment, jobs, new incomes, and prosperity with it. Today, money is migrating from the West to the East.

The money migration has five elements. In a moment, I'll show you how each leads to an investment opportunity, even though it may first appear to be a threat.

1. Welfare states in Europe and North America are going broke because they've made financial promises they can't keep.

2. Jobs and capital are moving from the highly regulated, high-wage, and high-tax economies of the West and Japan to Asia.

3. Competition for scarce natural resources is increasing. Supply is not.

4. The dollar standard is ending.

5. Investors have the power to respond to and profit from these trends.

The money migration is a way of explaining today's geopolitical world. Just as the societies of Europe and America and Japan reach retirement age, they find themselves confronted by fierce competition from India and China. This comes at a bad time for America, which has a great deal of debt. However, because of immigration and a relatively high birthrate (by industrialized standards), America's population, and thus its tax base, is not shrinking. Not so for Europe and Japan. Both are facing the demographic crisis of aging populations, low immigration, and birthrates that don't replace the dead. Europe and Japan are dying. The job of making things is migrating to Asia.

These internal crises are compounded as Europe, America, and Japan must now compete with newly industrializing countries for scarce resources. This competition is driving up prices in a wide range of commodities. But one thing not rising in price is the global cost of labor. Labor—skilled labor in India and manufacturing labor in China—is comparatively cheap next to labor in Europe, the United States, and Japan. American workers cannot compete with the wages their Asian competitors are willing to work for. So the jobs migrate.

The dollar standard is ending. The time when everyone wanted to own American stocks and bonds and America's currency is nearly at an end. But what will replace it? If jobs are moving east because labor costs are cheaper, and if capital is moving east because there are more new projects that promise higher returns on investment, where should you invest? What are the investment consequences of the money migration?

TWENTY-FIRST-CENTURY CAPITALISM

In thinking about Schumpeter's phrase, I realized that the most important investment riddle to solve over the next 10 years is figuring out just what makes a competitive and successful business in the twenty-first century. Which firms are strong enough to survive the challenges of globalization? Which ones are headed to the dustbin of history? Should you look for those firms in one part of the world more than another? Or will success have less to do with where you're located and more to do with what you do and how well you do it?

If you manage to make it through reckoning day with your capital intact, you'll have a world of choices. What I set out to discover last year were some signposts for the investment road ahead. I thought that by getting out from behind a desk and going to see what I'd been writing about for three years, I'd be able to chart a better investment course. When you see things for yourself, firsthand, you don't have to rely on anyone else's opinion.

In this chapter I'll give you the big-picture overview of what I saw. Before we pick the specific businesses we want to buy, we need to know the demands that have been created because of the money migration, what needs must be filled. It might turn out that it's easier and more profitable to invest in these trends using ETFs and index funds than through single stocks. Or it might not! You'll just have to read on and see.

Naturally, the investment picture and prospects for the future are different in every country. There are dangers as well. I'll tell you what to watch out for later.

More important, there are some common investment themes for each country—the need for food, fuel, and raw materials being the three big ones I observed. These themes are the basis of an investment strategy to profit from the money migration. In this chapter, I want to focus on the two very basic ones: energy and raw materials. In Chapter 6, we'll talk about others, including some general rules for investing in emerging markets. But first, let's look at the huge appetites that have been created by the money migration, and how to profit from them.

THE GLOBAL MINERAL GRAB IS ON

In the summer of 2004, while in China, I wrote the following:

> The Chinese have too much dollar exposure, both in the form of U.S. bonds and dollar currency reserves (over $100 billion in bonds and $300 billion in currency reserves). . . . I expect the Chinese might use some of those reserves to buy hard assets . . . like iron ore, or grains, or companies that own iron ore deposits . . . or farmland. . . . It's a truly strategic approach from the government . . . make deals with commodity-rich countries . . . and use dollar assets to secure your hard asset needs.[1]

I was predicting a form of the money migration, a way for China to lower its dollar risk and increase its net wealth at the same time. Since then, a distinct trend has emerged in global markets that confirms my early observation. Investors and countries with lots of dollars are desperately trading them for *real* assets. Consider the following developments:

- In late 2004, Chinese metal-trading giant China Minmetals Corp. made a bid for Noranda, Canada's largest miner and one of the world's leading producers of zinc and nickel and a major producer of copper, gold, and silver.

- Chinese companies invested $33 billion in 7,470 companies in over 160 countries in 2003, according to the Chinese Ministry of Commerce.

- China's Shanghai Automotive won a battle with China National Bluestar Corp. to buy Ssangyong Motor Co., South Korea's fourth largest automaker.

- Sanjiu Enterprise Group, China's biggest drug manufacturer, bought a majority stake in Toa Seiyaku Inc., a midsize Japanese pharmaceutical company.

A *China Post* article commented on the pattern, "Unlike Japanese purchases of French Impressionist masterpieces or showcase real estate in the late 1980s and early 1990s, China's deals have been low-profile and focused on stakes in vital resources: oil, gas, minerals, timber—even fish. More than 2,200 Chinese-owned fishing vessels ply the world's oceans." The strategy is clear. The *China Post* article continues, "After decades of struggling to prevent Chinese companies from spending precious foreign exchange overseas, Beijing is now pushing companies toward worldwide investments."[2] Is this part of China's deliberate, state-run economic policy? Surely it is. What's intriguing is that China is not alone in quietly getting out of dollar assets and into *real* assets. Take a look at other, similar developments:

- Russian steelmaker Severstal pays $286 million for Rouge Industries, the largest—and bankrupt—metal maker in the United States. Later it's revealed that Severstal will use its $1.4 billion war chest to buy bankrupt Canadian steelmaker Stelco.

- In 2003, Russian company Norilsk Nickel pays $255 million for Stillwater Mining, the last U.S. producer of platinum and palladium. Norilsk then pays $1.19 billion for Anglo American's 20 percent stake in South Africa's Gold Fields, the fourth biggest gold producer in the world.

- Russian president Vladimir Putin approves a merger between partially public gas producer Gazprom and state-owned oil company Rosneft. The new company has oil and gas reserves equivalent to 117 billion barrels of oil—five times the size of Exxon Mobil's reserves. It becomes the largest oil and gas company in the world that investors can buy.

- Mexican-based cement juggernaut CEMEX acquires British-based RMC Group, the world's largest supplier of ready-mix concrete, for 2.3 billion British pounds. It becomes the third largest cement company in the world, behind France's Lafarge and Switzerland's Holcim.

- South African gold producer Harmony makes a bid for Gold Fields Ltd. The bid competes with the proposed merger between Gold Fields and Canada's IAMGOLD, but is backed by Gold Field's shareholder Norilsk.

- Ispat International—controlled by Indian billionaire Lakshmi Mittal—announces it will acquire U.S.-based LNM Holdings for a $13.3 billion stock issue to LNM shareholders and merge International Steel Group for $4.5 billion in cash and stock.

Severstal has also said it will spend $140 million of its devaluing dollars rebuilding a real, income-producing, industrial-era asset: the coke ovens at the Follansbee site of Wheeling-Pittsburgh Steel Corp. It's not the first time a foreign firm has gleefully acquired a rusty American manufacturing asset. China's Wanxiang Group has been trolling the Midwest looking for more companies to add to a portfolio of American auto parts firms.

Let's stop a moment to take stock. The Russians and the Chinese—our former communist competitors—aren't racing out to buy Google. They're buying real assets all over the globe, even right here in America. These capital assets will help them compete globally. They'll also produce new income. The jobs have already moved. But some of the most important industrial machines and factories haven't. So foreign investors are showing up in America to buy those, too. It's a perfectly sensible strategy, if you're genuinely interested in long-term real economic growth.

Before you get too worried, this may bode well for certain U.S. industrial firms. These firms are hard to compete with because you cannot easily imitate what they do (more on that in Chapter 8). But take note: Communists, bankers, and politicians in China and Russia realize that in the future the best way to compete with America will be to buy its capital and industrial assets at a discount!

By now the point should be shockingly clear. Foreign governments, foreign corporations, and wealthy investors are using financial assets to acquire real assets. The shift out of paper and into stuff is on, and with a vengeance. What can you do as an investor?

START WITH ENERGY

The best place to start looking for investments in the booming hard-asset markets is in the energy markets. Granted, energy stocks had a great run in 2004 as crude oil futures rocketed to all-time highs. But you're interested in the long-term bull market going on in Asia. And as Asia grows, it's going to take energy to power it. If you need proof, take a look at one of the key companies in an already developed Asian workhorse, South Korea.

In 2004, *The Korea Herald* reported that Korea Electric Power (KEPCO) agreed to build two coal-fired power plants in China. China has some of the largest coal reserves in the world, even though it has little oil. The agreement was to build two 600-megawatt plants in Hunan province. In July 2003, KEPCO won a $71 million contract to build a 100-megawatt plant in the province.

There's no better example of voracious demand for energy than China (more on that in Chapter 6.) Electricity demand in China grew by 15 percent in 2003—twice as fast as its ability to generate new electric power. China needs to double its generating capacity from the current level of 400,000 megawatts to around 900,000 megawatts by 2008 to get ready for the Summer Olympics in Beijing (and to keep all those factories humming). To meet that demand, China plans to spend $8 billion to build four new nuclear reactors. The entire contract could go to one bidder—perhaps one that's already won the same kind of contract in the past, like KEPCO.

One of the best value investors I know, Dan Ferris, likes KEPCO for the quality of the assets it owns. I agree. As Dan shows, KEPCO's assets have fetched healthy multiples of book value over the last few years:

- Doosan Heavy Industries was carried on the books at 455.6 million won. It sold for $1.685 billion, *3.7 times book value.*
- KEPCO's 45.5 percent stake in Powercomm, a telecom subsidiary, sold for $707.99 million in 2002, *2.2 times book value* of $362.8 million.
- KEPCO sold 51 percent of KEPID in 2003. Book value of the 51 percent stake was 21 billion won. Proceeds were 71 billion won, or *3.4 times book.*

Dan points out that KEPCO's total assets up for sale have a book value of $1.3 billion. In his newsletter, *Extreme Value,* Dan wrote, "It's a simple exercise to apply the range of multiples KEPCO has received the past few years, i.e. between 2.2–3.7 times book value. That would value KEPCO's assets for sale at $2.86–4.8 billion. The upshot: Just 3% of KEPCO's total assets could sell for an amount equal to as much as 55% of KEPCO's outstanding long-term debt."[3] See Table 5.1.

Dan also makes a good point about value itself. One reason why

TABLE 5.1 KEPCO ASSETS UP FOR SALE ($ MILLIONS)

Company	Book Value	KEPCO Stake
KPS	$206.6	100%
KEPID	$17.3	49%
KDHC	$127.9	26.1%
KOGAS	$597.3	24.5%
KOPEC	$44.9	97.9%
Powercomm	$310.3	43.2%
Total:	$1.3 billion	

Source: *Extreme Value,* September 2004

certain heavy-industry, old-economy firms will do better than investors expect in the future is that they have durable assets. They can
compete even as China has fully emerged as the world's manufacturing workshop. "If these multiples seem a bit optimistic," Dan continues, "I understand." The best explanation for what's going on
with these valuations is in a book called *Value Investing From Graham
to Buffett and Beyond,* by Bruce Greenwald, et al. (John Wiley, 2004).
I quote from Chapter 4, titled "Valuing the Assets":

> If the industry is in serious decline, then the asset values of the company
> should be estimated based on what they will bring in liquidation. Since
> there will be no market for capital goods tailored to specific require-
> ments of the industry, they will basically be sold for scrap. On the other
> hand, if the industry is stable or growing, then the assets in use will need
> to be reproduced as they wear out. These assets should be valued at their
> reproduction cost.

At the time, Dan wrote, "If you apply the lowest multiple of
KEPCO's recent asset sales to its current book value per share,
KEPCO is worth five times what it's selling for today. KEPCO sells for
about 0.4 times book value today. Even if it took 10 years for the
price to reach the multiple I'm talking about (2.2 times book), you'd
still make 17.5% a year in pretax capital gains, on average. With the
S&P 500 at 2.95 times book, most U.S. stocks aren't priced to bring
you that kind of return."[4]

That may well have changed by the time you read this. But the
exercise is useful if you take away two lessons from it. First, find a good
investment theme. This is part of forming your strategy. Second, find
the best way to profit. This may mean buying a basket of stocks like an
ETF. Or it may mean doing some good old-fashioned balance sheet
analysis and buying a great individual company that can thrive in a
competitive world.

Either way, you'll have spotted a global opportunity and found a
specific way to profit from it. It's a process we'll repeat again in
Chapter 6. But we're not done with the energy markets yet. There's
another big story to be told, another big opportunity to be explored.

ENERGY INDEPENDENCE FOR NORTHEAST ASIA . . . AND NORTH AMERICA, TOO!

In late 2004, *The Japan Times* reported that Beijing gave several Chinese companies permission to conduct natural gas exploration in the East China Sea, an area the Japanese have long considered an exclusive economic zone. The Chinese also put pressure on Russian president Vladimir Putin in October to proceed with an $18 billion, 3,000-mile gas pipeline project from Russia's Kovykta Field in eastern Siberia to China's refiners to the south. The Chinese also pushed on a 1,500-mile link from western Siberia. Japan, meanwhile, is pushing for a pipeline from Vladivostok over the Sea of Japan.

Unmentioned was the big prize, the 18 trillion cubic feet of natural gas reserves that sit off the shore of Russia's Sakhalin Island. The island was a brutal and remote prison during the reign of Czar Alexander II. In fact, Russian poet and writer Anton Chekhov visited the island in 1890. After his visit, he wrote in a letter, "God's world is good. It is only we who are bad. . . . One must work, and to hell with everything else. The important thing is that we must be just and all the rest will come as matter of course . . ."[5]

The rest is coming to Sakhalin Island now, just God or no. The island is the energy mother lode of the region—a find rivaling Alaska's North Slope—and the kind of resource, if properly harnessed, that could power the region's energy needs for decades. It matters a great deal because the countries of northeast Asia are already vulnerable to disruptions in the flow of oil from the Persian Gulf. As Table 5.2 and Figure 5.1 show, China, South Korea, and Japan are already some of the world's largest oil importers. It's a precious energy lifeline that could easily be cut, either at the Strait of Hormuz or at another chokepoint, the Strait of Malacca.

How will a country like South Korea keep its powerhouse export-driven economy going without getting sucker punched by high oil prices? The answer is unknown. But continued development of its energy infrastructure—with companies like KEPCO—will help. Another answer may lie in liquid natural gas (LNG).

TABLE 5.2   TOP WORLD OIL NET IMPORTERS, 2003*

Country	Net Oil Imports (Million Barrels per Day)
1. United States	11.1
2. Japan	5.3
3. Germany	2.5
4. South Korea	2.2
5. China	2.0
6. France	2.0
7. Italy	1.7
8. Spain	1.5
9. India	1.4

*Table includes all countries that imported more than 1 million barrels per day in 2002.
Source: U.S. Department of Energy, Energy Information Administration

ENERGY'S LIQUID FUTURE

This is a golden age for oil and energy investments. Either that, or a fiery sunset that ends with oil and resource wars. But I prefer to look on the bright side. At the moment, however, the bright side of the oil and gas market is dimly lit. Continuous supply disruptions—

FIGURE 5.1   Strait of Malacca.
(Source: CIA, *The World Factbook,* www.cia.gov/cia/publications/factbook)

whether by acts of terrorists or acts of God—have altered traditional relationships between supply and demand, while also obliterating America's long-standing complacency about oil and gas supplies. Uncertainty reigns.

But amid the uncertain conditions of our changing petro-political world, liquid natural gas will certainly assume a prominent role. As I see it, there are two major opportunities in LNG: terminal construction and tanker construction. With LNG demand likely to rise from 120 million tonnes in 2003 to 200 million tonnes by 2010, and then 315 million tonnes by 2020 (according to estimates from the International Energy Agency), it's a question of getting the right mix of investments. But first a little background on the LNG market. The excellent *Plunkett's Energy Industry Almanac* for 2005 offers the following insights:

> One development as a result of higher [energy] price levels and increased demand is serious interest in supplying America's gas needs through LNG (liquefied natural gas). However, due to the necessity of special handling, bringing that supply online in a major quantity will take huge capital outlays and require considerable time. LNG requires special processing and transportation. First, the natural gas must be chilled to minus 260 degrees Fahrenheit, in order for it to change into a liquid state. Next, the LNG is put on specially designed ships where extensive insulation and refrigeration maintain the cold temperature. Finally, it is offloaded at special receiving facilities where it is converted into a state suitable for distribution via pipelines.[6]

Specially designed ships indeed! According to LNG Shipping Solutions, there were only 151 LNG tankers in operation in October 2003. And no wonder. Because of the rigorous specifications, the average cost of a 138,000-cubic-meter LNG tanker is about $160 million. According to the Energy Information Agency, that's more than double the price of a crude oil tanker that could carry four or five times as much energy.

Yet despite the cost and the seemingly bad comparison to oil tanker economics, there were 55 LNG tankers under construction as of last year. Forty-six of them are designed to carry 138,000 cubic meters of LNG, which translates into about 2.9 billion cubic feet of natural gas. LNG Shipping Solutions also notes that the ships currently under construction would raise the total fleet capacity by 44 percent, or from 17.4 million cubic feet of LNG (366 BcF of natural gas) to 25.1 million cubic meters of liquid (527 BcF of natural gas). See Figure 5.2.

But even with the increased capacity, Plunkett's says demand will keep rising enough to make looking at LNG-related investments worthwhile. Plunkett's continues:

> An analysis conducted in late 2003 by the National Petroleum Council projected that the U.S. could meet as much as 14% of its natural gas needs through LNG imports by 2025, if sufficient infrastructure were built, including seven new LNG transportation facilities. Transporting LNG from distant countries presents massive technological and financial challenges, but importing LNG from those nations could provide much needed gas for the U.S., assuming America is willing to add to its already bloated import bills and balance of payment problems.[7]

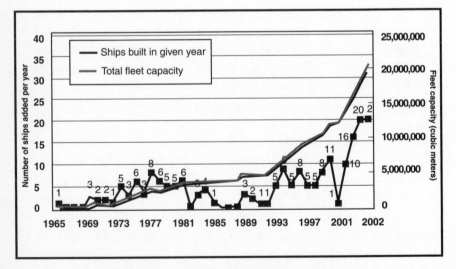

FIGURE 5.2 Hockeystick growth in LNG shipping.
(Source: LNG Shipping Solutions)

One of the biggest barriers to wider use of LNG in the United States is a lack of terminals to receive it. Plunkett's elaborates:

> On the receiving side, the special terminals in the U.S. dedicated to LNG have been limited to four on the mainland and one in Puerto Rico. Many of these plants have been expanded in recent years. Even though these reception facilities are expensive, costing $400 to $600 million each and taking more than three years to build, the biggest barrier to establishing new terminals has been concern over their safety, concerns which were aggravated by a recent explosion of an LNG plant in Algeria which killed 27 people.[8]

California is already witnessing a fight between those who see the benefits of cheap natural gas and those who don't want LNG terminals built offshore. But let's assume for a moment the cheap energy interests will win out over the NIMBY interests. Who will make all these new LNG terminals? And who will make the ships to transport the LNG from the rich gas fields of the world to the hungry energy markets of Asia and America? First, Plunkett's conclusion:

> The LNG business is already booming. Growth will continue as oil companies and oil-rich countries realize the benefit of transporting gas in liquid form. LNG technology is moving ahead rapidly, and costs for transporting it are coming down. Shipping and handling will become more competitive as more ships and facilities come into operation, and large quantities of LNG on the market could stabilize or even depress natural gas prices.
>
> Many markets outside the U.S. are also prime targets for LNG imports, including China and India. Japan is already a huge importer of LNG, there being little other way to transport gas to the island country . . . the United States contains vast quantities of natural gas in areas that currently cannot be exploited. The U.S. Geological Survey estimates that there are 1,400 trillion cubic feet of recoverable natural gas in the U.S., which would be enough to power the nation for decades. Most of this gas lies beneath regulated federal and state lands (particularly in Rocky Mountain basins, offshore America's east and west coasts

and offshore the west coast of Florida), much of which cannot be drilled upon under present regulations.

Environmental and regulatory concerns may mean that most of this gas will never be produced, unless economic imperatives intervene. . . . For the mid-term, gas will remain in great demand, and prices will tend to be high. While there is significant additional gas to be found in the Gulf of Mexico, such projects take years to bring online. "Meanwhile, the largest potential exporters of natural gas to the U.S. are those countries with the largest proven reserves: Russia, Iran, Qatar, Saudi Arabia, Algeria, Venezuela, Nigeria, Iraq and Indonesia, in that order.[9]

LNG INVESTMENT FUTURE

If you take a look at Plunkett's list of countries, and if you're anything like me, you're probably pretty uncomfortable making investments in Qatar, Saudi Arabia, Venezuela, Nigeria, and Iraq. But the good news is, you don't have to.

The best game in town for LNG terminal construction is U.K.-based BG Group plc, which trades as an American Depository Receipt (ADR) on the New York Stock Exchange under the symbol BRG. BG Group is what you'd call an integrated natural gas company, which means it operates in five separate areas of the natural gas industry: exploration, production, LNG, transmission and distribution, and power generation. BG also managed to become the leading provider of LNG to the United States by developing four gas fields in Trinidad and Tobago, of all places. It has a 26 percent stake in the Trinidad and Tobago LNG facility that currently supplies the majority of LNG to the United States. It also owns part of two U.S. import terminals.

With BG and other major oil and gas companies just beginning to develop LNG terminals and gas fields all over the world, the second place to look at future investment opportunities is in the LNG shipping business. That brings us directly to South Korea, which has the good fortune of being in the heart of one of the most energy-ravenous regions of the world. It also has some of the most successful LNG ship makers in the world, a list that includes

- Hyundai Heavy Industries
- Daewoo Shipbuilding and Marine Engineering
- Samsung Heavy Industries

These are the first, second, and third largest shipbuilders in the world, respectively. Together, these three companies captured 90 percent of all LNG ship orders in the first seven months of 2004, for a total of 29 ships. In fact, on Monday, October 11, 2004, the government of Qatar announced a deal with Daewoo to build 4 LNG ships. And Exxon Mobil was expected to buy 16 LNG ships as part of XOM's partnership with the emir of Qatar to develop Qatar's gas resources.

You can expect more deals like that in the future. Building LNG ships is complicated. For example, if you poured liquefied gas into a steel tank, it would shatter like glass. LNG ships are made of the kind of materials that can keep the gas cool once it's been liquefied, which involves thick aluminum, nickel steel, and balsa wood (for insulation). It's an art the South Koreans have perfected. And you can expect the South Korean shipbuilders to profit handsomely.

As the petro-political map of the world evolves, we'll be keeping a close eye on LNG. But the entire energy complex is in a strong bull market. Another way to invest is to go long some of those oil- and energy-related ETFs and index funds we discussed earlier. It wouldn't surprise me a bit if you can soon buy a crude oil or natural gas ETF the same way you can now buy gold.

RESOURCE WARS?

Demand for energy, raw materials, and real assets is clearly booming. There will be quiet periods. But these are strong fundamental trends, driven by the money migration and the rise of the East. Yet the rise of China and India, the race for resources, and the threat of oil wars all seem like ominous events for investors. And it may turn out to be that way for some investors—those who ignore large trends the way you would try to ignore gravity.

When I was young, I remember watching a wall of water wash down the main street of my hometown in Estes Park, Colorado. An earthen dam containing Lawn Lake in Rocky Mountain National Park had burst at around 5:30 in the morning on July 15, 1982. A man named Steve Gillette was collecting trash at a campground nearby and heard the sound of the water rushing down from 11,000 feet, toward the Estes Valley, at 7,500 feet and about 10 miles away. He called ahead to warn folks in town.

Take the potential energy of 29 million gallons of water. Turn it into kinetic energy filled with boulders the size of houses and fallen trees. Steve Gillette saved a lot of lives by providing a warning. He was jokingly referred to as the Paul Revere of Estes Park. But it was a well-intentioned joke.

Most of us don't have to worry about natural disasters. The December 2004 tsunami in Asia proved they still happen, though. If you get caught up in one, there's not much you can do at that point. Human beings are clever and have figured out many ways to tame nature's danger. But it still sometimes gets the best of us.

Financial disasters, however, are avoidable. Even large financial forces like the money migration that seem to sneak up on other investors like a sudden storm can be planned for and turned into opportunities rather than threats. There's no need to be caught by surprise. But you have to be willing to go beyond a superficial understanding of what's driving those forces in order to see your way through them clearly.

THE WAGES OF SIN

Money goes where it gets the highest return. For the last 20 years, everyone in the world has wanted to own U.S. stocks and bonds. We haven't had to work too hard to keep the money flowing in. The high returns in the stock market and the relative safety of the bond market did that.

But poor performance in the stock market and high government debts are lessening the attraction of American stocks and bonds. And meanwhile, confidence in America's financial markets themselves has been eroded. When the reckoning day does come, a lot of the fictitious, credit-financed wealth in America will be destroyed—especially in the housing and government bond markets.

As Mephistopheles says in Goethe's *Faust*, "Everything that rises goes rightly to its ruin." Big things don't last forever, especially when they got big by gorging on cheap credit and reckless speculation. The moral equivalent of gravity is sin. Both involve falling. Reckless investors will find out that there are consequences to spending more than you can pay back and intentionally misleading shareholders and investing in financial assets instead of real assets.

America's financial economy will be destroyed, and a lot of capital will be lost. But creation and destruction go hand in hand. What sets in the West rises in the East. The money migration will lead to the creation of a new economy and new wealth, perhaps on a scale far greater than we can imagine.

The world keeps turning, too. The sun never really goes down on investors who look for good value and invest along with powerful trends. There will still be plenty of opportunity in America as well. There already is. In Chapter 9, I'll show you where.

CHAPTER 6

THE DRAGON IN THE PIN-STRIPED SUIT

The Chinese will eat anything on four legs except tables and chairs, anything that swims except a submarine, and anything that flies except an airplane.

—Cantonese saying

Something is missing in Beijing's Forbidden City. You pass through the Meridian Gate, cross over one of the five bridges that span the Golden Water, go through the Gate of Supreme Harmony and across the 30,000-square-meter Harmony Square, on your way to the Hall of Supreme Harmony.

In 1911, that's where the last emperor of China was confined after the Forbidden City was occupied by the revolutionary forces of Dr. Sun Yat-sen, the father of modern China. You may not have heard of him, but he's more revered in China, among some, than Mao. It wouldn't surprise me if that trend continues in the future. But let's return to the past for just a moment.

By the time China's 2,000-year-old imperial dynasty fell, the Forbidden City had already been looted by the French and British 50 years earlier. If the city looks spartan, it's partly by design and partly by theft.

In the 1830s, riding the waves of England's growing industrial and maritime dominance, Britain's East India Company exported tons of opium to China. The British traded the opium for tea and manufactured goods. As you might expect, Britain's opium dumping on the Chinese market had disastrous social consequences. China's imperial government (Qing Empire) made opium illegal in 1836 and began closing down opium dens throughout China.

The British were not pleased. They spent two years running their gunships up and down China's eastern coast, bombarding the emperor into submission. In 1842 the Treaty of Nanking reopened the opium trade and exempted British citizens from Chinese law. Two years later, France and the United States signed similar treaties with China. The war planted historic seeds of resentment that still flower today.

The first opium war forcibly opened up China for free trade, especially for opium. A new war broke out in the period from 1856 to 1860. This time, the British and French united under one command and pressed for an even greater advantage. They were joined by Russia and the United States, which was about to have domestic problems of its own.

In the second opium war the Western powers succeeded in driving the emperor from his palace in Peking and occupying the city. The eventual settlement of the war opened up 10 more Chinese ports to trade, made it permissible for foreign ships (including warships) to navigate the Yangtze River, allowed Chinese workers the right to work overseas, gave foreigners the right to travel inside China, and granted Christians the right to own property and proselytize. The West forcibly opened China's vast internal market to the outside world, and did it on Western terms.

Today, China has begun exacting a measure of economic revenge for the rough treatment it received at the hands of the West. It has flooded Western markets with cheap manufactured goods. Shopping has become the opiate of the American masses. The Chinese are not content to simply sell textiles and electronics to America. Their ambition is to turn China into the world's next great economic superpower.

Getting there means developing China's vast internal market. Already there are 200 million consumers in China's middle class. In this chapter, we'll look at what the development of that internal market means for investors and the strategy China has used to pull itself up by the hair from the muddy backwaters of communism into an industrialized economy. Finally, we'll look at the political, economic, and social risks China faces in becoming the great power it aspires to be.

One last note: I'm not an expert on China. As I said earlier, spending a few weeks in a country—especially a country like China with thousands of years of history—can't make you an expert. But you can talk to people, read, and make up your own mind. That is, in fact, what you do when you decide to make an investment. You gather information, observe the world around you, talk to people who can provide you with insight and perspective you don't have, and then make up your own mind. (If you are interested in reading more about it and seeing some pictures I took while on my three-month trip to Asia, please visit www.eastprofits.blogspot.com.)

CHINA'S CAPITAL STRATEGY

When I arrived in Hong Kong, I was preceded by the most famous bull in the world, Michael Jordan. MJ was in town for only a few hours, to promote a line of clothing that was being manufactured in Hong Kong and sold all over the world, including mainland China.

Some economists have begun to complain that China is actually growing too fast and investing too much. The chief concern is that the Chinese have overinvested in fixed capital. More specifically, China has imported inflation from the United States by fixing its currency to the U.S. dollar. Credit excesses in the United States lead to rising asset prices and consumption. In China, they lead, so the theory goes, to reckless bank lending and overproduction of manufactured goods. China is building too many factories?!

Before we try to decide whether having too many factories producing too much stuff is really a problem (or a worse problem than having not enough factories at all), let's look at the numbers. China's fixed investment spending is equal to about 43 percent of its GDP as of 2003 (latest available). That's a high percentage. According to the CIA *World Factbook*,[1] it's the seventh highest percentage of 145 nations surveyed. You might be interested to know that Equatorial Guinea is first, with a percentage of 63.6 percent. That, too, is a high number. But it's relative to a GDP of $1.27 billion. (The United States comes in at 122nd, with about 15 percent of GDP going to fixed capital investment.)

China's investment in fixed assets for the first eight months of 2004 was around $402 billion, according to official government statistics. That turns into an annual rate of about $600 billion, or roughly 40 percent of China's $1.5 trillion GDP. That's *after* the government rolled back about $100 billion in bank lending for fixed assets in April.

But is it too much? Or, in economic terms, can a government efficiently and productively manage the task of investing $600 billion a year in fixed capital projects? Or is it inevitably going to lead to bubbles and overinvestment in certain sectors (hint: the ones that favor the bankers or government officials)?

Again going to the data, we see that 25 percent of China's investment in fixed assets is in manufacturing. No surprise there. But that does not, de facto, constitute a bubble. China's National Bureau of Statistics lists 30 separate categories of fixed-asset investment in manufacturing. No single manufacturing category accounts for more than 3.5 percent of total fixed investment (ferrous metal smelting commands the largest percentage, at 3.5 percent).

If you look at the growth rates of investment in particular sectors, you get an idea of where China's planners think China's needs lie. Investment in ferrous metal mining grew 256 percent in the first eight months of this year compared to last. Oil processing, coking plants, and nuclear material processing grew by 127.5 percent. Wood processing investment was up 71 percent, furniture manufacturing investment was up 52 percent, and general metal products investment was up 57.4 percent.

China, it appears, is trying to turn itself into a steel superpower. When you see the internal growth projects later, you'll see why. But the important point now is that these are the investment priorities of an industrializing nation. There's really nothing shocking about any of the numbers you see here. In fact, the deeper you dig, the more you'll see signs that China is using its $54 billion in annual foreign direct investment deliberately and pragmatically. It's building itself an industrial base on the back of Western capital. Not bad for a nation that didn't have a lot of capital to begin with.

When you can leverage your single indigenous economic advantage—abundant labor—to create a currency policy that makes your goods perpetually cheap to the world's most voracious consumers *and* manage to get Western investors to build factories for you, you've been either lucky or clever, or both. China is building its economic base with the benefit of foreign capital. But once the base is built, it will be China's. The state, after all, is the largest landowner. And there is no private property.

The fixed capital investment numbers show more of the same the deeper you dig. Investment in transportation was 11.5 percent of all fixed-asset spending. Road construction made up 7.6 percent of all investment. New water projects, such as the Three Gorges Dam, made up 8.2 percent. These are simple needs for a massive country. More water. More energy. More roads. More iron. More steel.

The Chinese are importing factories, roads, dams, and the entire industrial infrastructure of a developed economy. They're doing it quickly. And though there will surely be some mistakes and some corruption, they will have real assets capable of producing a large variety of goods and services.

Now, it's possible, in a global bust (led by the radical decline in American standards of living and per capital income), that China won't have anyone to sell anything to. But I doubt that. For one thing, China's best customers in the future will be other Asians and the Chinese people themselves. But secondly, even in a global bust, China will still have its fixed assets when the next cyclical boom comes around. An idle factory gets rusty. But you can scrape off the rust and get it going again. Having rusty factories is a better problem than, say, having spent most of your business investment on software that's no longer useful.

Why do I mention software? In 2003, there was $1.6 trillion in private fixed investment in the United States. The bulk of that ($1 trillion) was business investment. And of that, nearly 60 percent, or $596 billion, was spent on software and computer equipment. There's no doubt, as Fed chairman Greenspan has often reminded us, that information technology (IT) spending, in some nebulous way, does lead to greater productivity. And in that sense, IT and software investment produce obvious economic benefits.

They do not, however, produce a multitude of new jobs. And to the extent that productivity per worker actually increases, it eventually and inevitably must lead to fewer workers. It has to follow that the more productive an employee is because of a piece of software, the fewer employees you need to do that job (if the job itself hasn't already been outsourced).

U.S. businesses are investing in assets that reduce the need to pay high wages to large numbers of employees. China is investing in factories that make things. The United States is investing in technologies that may make services more efficient and better for the consumer, but in economic terms may mean lower average wages for most people in the workforce.

That's not to say that it's bad for U.S. business to invest in software and IT that improve efficiency or productivity. Productivity increases are essential to economic growth. They allow a firm to raise profits without raising wages. It's income without the expense. And over time, it's how we all get richer.

But it's not just the national income statement that we ought to be paying attention to. It's the balance sheet. Is American business investing in assets that produce wealth and create jobs? Certainly. But does fixed capital investment in software spread the same large macroeconomic benefits as fixed investment in, say, a power plant?

Perhaps the question is unfair. After all, China and the United States have different labor forces, are worlds apart in terms of economic maturity, and would naturally have different investment needs. On that we could all probably agree.

And we might agree on two other statements. First, regardless of the economic benefits of investment in software and IT, U.S. business investment has been poor and driven more by financial speculation made possible through the easy-money, low-rate largesse of the Federal Reserve.

Second, despite whatever short-term busts the Chinese reap from overinvesting in productive capacity, the long-term benefit is that they have migrated the productive capacity of the world to their shores. It should stay there for a long, long time. Besides, China will need that capacity as its internal market develops. That development, however, won't be easy.

MEGACITIES VERSUS NATURE

China is the story that matters most if you're asking what the world will look like the day after reckoning day. In the short term, you've got a bank system loaded down with bad debts and overinvestment in commercial real estate. But you've also got a country consuming half the world's cement, with a voracious demand for iron ore and other raw materials. That demand might slow down by command, through higher interest rates to contain inflation. Or it might go through normal free-market booms and busts. But it's not anywhere close to letting up.

In Hong Kong, I listened to a speech by Paul Cheng, who used to run the Chamber of Commerce in Hong Kong. Mr. Cheng laid out 10 Chinese megatrends. I won't go through all of them here. But I'll give you two. One boggles the mind. One sobers it up.

The first is the urbanization of China. Mr. Cheng estimates that with about 300 million upwardly mobile middle-class Chinese, China's eastern coast could sprout between 10 and 20 new cities with populations of 15 to 30 million people. My first question when I heard this was, "Is it even possible?" If China is already consuming a huge portion of the world's raw materials—especially iron ore from Brazil, Australia, and India—where will the money and material come from to build 20 new megacities?

DEMOGRAPHIC DANGER

This brings us to Mr. Cheng's sobering prediction. China has a demographic problem, too. The population is getting old without first having gotten rich, to paraphrase an article by Nick Eberstadt published in *Policy Review*.[2] How long can China sustain its competitive advantage as a manufacturing haven? If you're looking strictly at the labor pool, quite a long time.

But an aging workforce that's been used hard in labor-intensive jobs—and an environment that's been used even harder—impose indirect costs on the economy. Those costs catch up with the society sooner or later. In the labor market, they catch up in higher health care costs. Right now, the government is not equipped to meet the costs of caring for an aging population. This could mean privatization—and investment opportunity. It could also be a huge risk to China's progress forward—an enormous unfunded social welfare liability.

Unregulated industrial development—with a high degree of pollution of the air and water—is an indirect subsidy to industry at the expense of the health of the population. When you don't have to clean up after yourself, there's less pressure on profit margins.

How China handles this development will be interesting to watch. It's possible that high unemployment and a portion of the population that doesn't feel like it's benefiting from growing prosperity are sources of political trouble. But that wouldn't make China any different from Germany, France, or the United States. China's problems are manageable, and China is developing more internal institutions to handle its rapid economic growth.

A good example is the emergence of commodity and futures exchanges. China has the Dalian Commodity Exchange, which is the second largest soybean futures market in the world. Last year the state council that currently oversees futures trading just gave the green light for cotton futures to trade on the Zhengzhou Commodity Exchange. In Shanghai, the futures exchange is moving into currencies and got approval to trade oil futures back in April.

Futures exchanges are popping up all over Asia. They're not going to compete with the major futures exchanges in the West anytime soon. But that's not the point. The point is to allow domestic producers of raw materials a more liquid way to hedge their risk and establish a niche futures market at the same time.

The state is worried about the speculation that futures markets can incite. It's even rattled sabers about foreign speculators keeping money locked up in banks, waiting for yuan revaluation, instead of investing in Chinese securities. But the bluster aside, the opening up of the futures markets is a good sign, especially if the gold exchange in Shanghai moves into the futures market. For now, even trading spot gold is bullish for the "relic." Volume is still small on the exchange. I saw that firsthand when I walked on the floor and chatted with some of the traders.

It's the concept that's big. The traders I talked to in Shanghai say the big source of gold demand in China is industrial—mostly for China's growing automobile industry. The Shanghai exchange is a way for industrial consumers of gold to hedge risk. Personally, I think China needs food more than it needs cars. There is not enough oil in the world to fuel more cars in China.

What's happening in China is the emergence of hundreds of millions of people into the global marketplace as both consumers and producers. There will be booms and busts in Chinese stocks. But for truly long-term investors, anything that profits from the development of Chinese infrastructure, financial services, and health services is the best way to profit from development inside China.

For example, take Australian mining giant BHP Billiton (BHP). You'd be hard-pressed to find a better China proxy than BHP. BHP knows the demand for raw materials in Asia is a multiyear boom. Last year, BHP announced plans to increase its metallurgical coal production in the next 10 years. It's going to cost the company some $2 billion—not chump change. But then, the profits won't be, either. Metallurgical coal is the kind of coal that is converted to coke for manufacturing steel. Anyone, or any country, that wants to produce more steel needs more metallurgical coal. BHP happens to be the world's largest supplier of seaborne metallurgical coal (it produces about 58 million metric tons today).

With official estimates that Chinese demand for steel is expected to grow by 20 million tons a year for the next five years, the Chinese are going to need a lot of metallurgical coal and iron ore. BHP, shipping from Australia, is in the right place at the right time.

China realized well before India that unleashing domestic demand was the key to having a balanced economy, not just an economy that relied on a cheap currency to finance competitive exports. In

Chapter 7, you'll see how the Indians have realized this now, too. That also means keeping an eye on local companies making money in India. In Chapter 9, I'll show you some simple rules to keep in mind when investing in emerging markets. But it shouldn't be surprising that China and India should see rising domestic consumption. After all, the Chinese want to live the good life, too, not just provide it to Americans at a discount. Savings rates are high in China. But there are major trends powering domestic consumption. A whole new nation-in-waiting is poised to move out of low-paying agricultural jobs in the hinterlands into higher-wage jobs in China's urban centers. The first and most obvious demand is going to be for extensive urban infrastructure: water, electricity, roads, rails, and airports.

But as living standards rise in China, it suddenly becomes an investment market in its own right, a place where you want to sell and not just make. It will take years for average living standards in China to rise to Western levels, if, in fact, that's even possible in a nation of over 1.3 billion people. But even if GDP per capita in China lags the West for years, there will still be immense GDP growth fueled by domestic demand.

SO WHAT ARE THE RISKS?

A key concern for China is the soundness of its capital markets—especially the banking system. But China (like much of Asia) is moving toward more intra-Asian trade based on Asian savings, both personal and corporate. The trend away from debt capitalization toward equity continues to grow, even to accelerate. It's the kind of structural rebalancing I had in mind when I came up with the idea of the money migration.

The government is turning over more and more control of the economy to market forces. Two of the big four state banks are cleaning up their balance sheets in preparation for IPOs in the United States. The banks are selling off nonperforming assets—especially commercial real estate loans—in order to raise cash and get the loans off the books.

For example, while I was in China, the China Construction Bank sold off $169 million in commercial real estate assets. The sale came at a 34 percent discount on the face value of the assets, which included a 31-story office tower and 400,000 square feet of office space. This is great news as just a financial story. The bank is tackling its bad loan problem by selling off assets. That's something that still seems to be a problem in Japan. The Chinese are dealing with it directly.

But the bigger fact is that since the bank is the state, this amounts to the privatization of the credit business. The state is selling off its assets to raise cash. It's gradually turning over finance and banking to the private sector. This encourages investment. When the government allows profit, capital and money migrate. Firms are starting to size up the Chinese market as a place to sell into.

A 2004 study in Japan's *Daily Yomiuri* newspaper reported that of 413 Japanese firms surveyed, 68 percent said they considered China a major export market as well as a manufacturing base. Go five years out and 90 percent figure China to be a major export market. China is rapidly advancing as both a major exporter and a global consumer. This is bullish for both China *and* commodity prices, especially food, as you'll see in Chapter 7.

RISKS TO THE DRAGON'S SERENE FUTURE

China faces an enormous test, the like of which is new in history: how to manage the transition of hundreds of millions of people from subsistence-level, labor-intensive farming to labor-intensive manufacturing done from cities with 15 million people. It's a mass migration no government could possibly manage. One way or another, the market will have to manage it. But the free market is not a school-crossing officer or social worker. It does not wait to make sure every last person keeps up.

China's transition is likely to be volatile and, in human terms, awfully difficult to manage for the old, the infirm, and those without savings or a family network. Then again, China has a 5,000-year history of Confucian and Taoist teachings in its cultural DNA. Those native institutions of social organization may help it through what would otherwise be a demographic catastrophe.

Growing quickly when you're enormous to begin with is not without very real risks. Investors who think making money in Chinese stocks will be an easy matter are mistaken. Everyone knows the story of China's miracle growth. But if you spend a few hours in any major Chinese city, you'll see that growth has had some unintended consequences. I mentioned to you before that I was shocked at how poor the air quality in China was during my visit. It wasn't a seasonal phenomenon. For example, there are now over 160 days a year when visibility in Hong Kong is less than five miles.

The culprits are factories in Shenzhen. But don't expect poor air quality to slow down Chinese demand for raw materials. For example, a recent Goldman Sachs report states that iron ore prices may increase to $28.53 a ton due to rising Chinese demand. This validates our strategy of China profits without the China risk—namely, buying the Western companies doing business with China and taking a pass at speculating on U.S.-listed shares of Chinese companies. Why?

Cherry-picking the winning Chinese companies on U.S. markets is a gamble. You can make money at it, but you can also get burned when white-hot speculative demand gives way to misplaced skepticism. The fundamental economic story in China is the mass migration of hundreds of millions of rural farmers to the urban coast to create a vast internal market. That's where a discussion of risks and opportunities should begin.

The good news is that more and more of the planning in China is being turned over to the marketplace for the simple reason that the marketplace does a much better job than the state. Free markets work better than governments. The bad news is that free markets do less well at solving other problems, such as the aging of China's population—a population that will need better food, shelter, and medical care. Where will that money come from? Or is there *already* too much money floating in China's capital markets?

A CHINA BUBBLE?

If there is a bubble caused by easy credit and bad bank lending, it's in commercial real estate, which constitutes 25 percent of all fixed capital investment. This is one of the risks to China's growth that I'll discuss later on. But it also explains why Shanghai's skyline looks so much like Hong Kong's. Jiang Zemin (the former president of the People's Republic of China) had his political base in Shanghai, and all his political allies are in the region. Shanghai was quite consciously built up as a mainland version of Hong Kong (there are 626 high-rise buildings in Shanghai).

As I mentioned, the commercial real estate portfolios of China's large banks are being sold off at a loss (the main real estate lenders being the Industrial and Commercial Bank of China and the China Construction Bank). The government wants to clean up these bank balance sheets so that the banks can go public.

The word in banking circles (at least from friends of mine in London) is that in order to clean up those balance sheets, the government will also inject a huge amount of cash to bulk up reserves. This defeats the purpose of getting the government out of the commercial real estate lending business, if it's simply going to subsidize the banks directly.

The longer-term question for China is how long it will take the capital markets to mature so that bank lending isn't the major source of capital for investment. Will China's equity markets grow? Will there be a bond market? Will the commodities and futures exchanges take root? And what about Taiwan?

STRATEGIC RISK IN TAIWAN

The biggest risk I see in China right now is not economic, but political. And what's more, China's biggest risk is itself and how it might act if Taiwan pushes for a two-state relationship.

Personally, I don't think the United States is willing to go to war over Taiwan. American interests in the region are more economic than military. For their part, though, the Chinese seem deadly serious about Taiwan. In fact, everyone I talked to in China was unanimous that China would not and could not allow Taiwan independence. China will go to war over Taiwan if it has to. How might that war play out? Dr. Marc Faber sets the stage:

Wendell Minnick, who is the Jane's *Defense Weekly* correspondent for Taiwan, sets a likely scenario. According to Minnick, should China ever decide to invade Taiwan, it would unlikely be a large-scale, Normandy-type of amphibious assault, but be by means of a "decapitation strategy." Minnick explains that "Decapitation strategies short-circuit command and control systems, wipe out nationwide nerve centers, and leave the opponent hopelessly lost. As the old saying goes, 'Kill the head and the body dies.' "[3]

If this assessment is accurate, China's Taiwan strategy is not at all different from the U.S. strategy of "shock and awe" in Iraq. It's a variation on the idea of getting inside your adversary's decision cycle. We'll take a closer look at how you can apply that to the stock market in Chapter 9. In military terms, it means attacking in unexpected ways and in unexpected places (not strictly military targets). By doing so, you get your opponent off balance. By the time they react to what you've done, you're doing another thing, eventually collapsing their will to resist by the speed and ubiquity of your assault.

The Chinese have played their Taiwan hand beautifully. With the United States engaged in Iraq and dependent on China and Russia to disarm North Korea, it looks to me like a reuniting of Taiwan and the mainland may simply be a matter of time. Whether it's by peaceful means or not remains to be seen.

It also remains to be seen whether the United States considers it more important to support Taiwan's ambitions rather than to make nice with mainland China and its growing economy and huge holdings of U.S. bonds. In his 2005 inaugural address, President George W. Bush said, "It is the policy of the United States to seek and support the growth of democratic governments and institutions in every nation and culture, with the ultimate goal of ending tyranny in our world." An ambitious goal, to say the least, and one that must include Taiwan.

It's hard to imagine, with $124 billion in trade between them and their economic futures now intimately intertwined, that America and China would go to war over Taiwan. But both appear determined to do just that if they feel they have to. Let's hope they don't have to.

There's also the possibility—which would be even more shock-ing—that the mainland Chinese communist leadership will collapse *before* China ever attacks Taiwan. How could this happen? In late January 2005, Zhao Ziyang died. Zhao was the leader of the Com-munist Party in 1989 during the student uprisings in Tiananmen Square. He spent the last 15 years of his life under house arrest for hav-ing refused to order a crackdown on the pro-democracy demonstra-tors. He was mourned by thousands in Hong Kong, where it is still legal to gather in public and support democracy.

In mainland China, nothing of the sort could happen. When I strolled through Tiananmen Square, it was not too hard to notice the plainclothes police who still follow Westerners, in addition to uni-formed police. My guide in Beijing made sure to remind me not to bring up the subject in public. Despite outward appearances of pros-perity, China is not democratic.

Yet there *is* a chance that the mainland could become more like Taiwan, and not the other way around. It has to do with the connec-tion between economic prosperity and liberty, a subject I'll touch on in Chapter 9. For now, let me quote a friend of mine who currently lives in Taiwan and describes himself as a pro-free-market libertarian:

> Taiwan cannot be free and secure, if China is not free and democratic. And, as China goes, so goes Asia. Whether China becomes a super-power or descends into another period of warlordism, things will not stay as they are (although I have not yet been to the mainland), and the rest of Asia and the world will be impacted, to say the least. It would be difficult for anyone to convince me that China's transition will occur in as sweet a fashion as did the Soviet Union's. . . . I believe that Taiwan is correct to push forward the controversial name changes to state-run industries. Taiwan's only chance is to continually let the world know the true nature of the Chinese beast. It is simply inconceivable how anybody could object to Taiwan's right to self-determination. However, there is a danger in accelerating the Taiwanization of the ROC, namely that there are still very powerful elements within Taiwan that are attached to the idea of a China one and indivisible. More needs to be done to make the emerging pro-independence government broadly representative. Not only because it is right, but because it will

make Taiwan stronger internally, it will give China fewer excuses to interfere in Taiwanese affairs, and it will set an example not only for China, but an example to the rest of Asia, how democracy can be reconciled with order. . . . [T]his is perhaps overly kind to the Chinese view, there is some reason for them to fear democracy.

Needless to say, a Chinese invasion of Taiwan would be a shock to financial markets. But given the ways in which the Chinese might accomplish such an invasion, and making the large assumption that the United States will offer only diplomatic resistance, I think the shock would be short-lived and not substantial. In the meantime, the best way to invest in China is to buy the companies doing business with China but that have Western listings.

It's a huge paradox. China has all the artifacts of a modern capitalist economy. And its people and entrepreneurs are a lot more opportunistic than many Americans I know. Yet little is known of the millions Mao killed. And while not as visible, the military is a constant reminder of the coercive nature of the Chinese state. For all its remarkable progress toward free markets, there has been a lot less progress toward freely expressed political thought. Can the government maintain its grip on information? Can it privatize nearly every other sector but keep a tight rein on what people say and publish? I doubt it.

The Chinese I met on my trip were bright, talented, ambitious people. They are also very proud of China. It will be their job to clean up the heinous mistakes of the state over the last 50 years. The Chinese government's war on the family has left hundreds of millions without a traditional support network as they get older. There are no institutions to fill the void. Not the state, which can't afford it. Not the church, which doesn't exist in large enough numbers. And not the family, which was systematically eliminated by the one-child policy.

Then again, Chinese culture is 5,000 years old. Communists can ruin a lot in a short time. Nothing is more destructive than the conceit that you can dispose of hundreds of years of tradition and evolution and replace it with a crackpot, egoistic, planned economy. But Buddhist, Taoist, and Confucian thought and beliefs are still at the heart of China. Not even an all-powerful state could eradicate that.

How else to explain that Sun Yat-sen, the father of the Chinese nation, is more popular than Mao? His mausoleum in Nanjing is a shrine of sorts. I went there myself and discussed his legacy with several of the Chinese I traveled with. Mao was feared, but he made China great. Sun Yat-sen is revered, and he makes the Chinese proud.

My prediction: *As China moves into center stage in the world economy, its traditional culture and its emerging free-market culture will replace the statist culture.* It will be better for China and the world. The state may be planning otherwise, but it can't control what it's unleashed. And for that, we should all be grateful. China is a beautiful place with kind, hardworking people. The real moneymaking there has just begun, and it's spreading throughout Asia like fire in a crowded theater.

A CHINA STRATEGY FOR THE FUTURE

Chinese companies with transparent financial statements and real earnings *may* start coming public in the United States in the near future. All you have to do is wait. In the meantime, there's nothing to prevent you from looking into the leading grain, iron ore, and commodity companies doing business with China.

What's happening in China is not a simple financial asset bubble. *It's the emergence of hundreds of millions of people into the global marketplace as both consumers and producers.* Truly long-term investors can profit from the development of Chinese infrastructure, financial services, and health services.

There are large appetites in China. Less than 100 years after the end of the feudal system, and less than 30 years after the communists opened up to the West again, China is clearly open for business. It has huge needs. Who will meet them? How can you profit?

CHAPTER 7

BOMBAY DREAMS AND ECONOMIC REALITY IN INDIA

In India, nothing is as it seems.

—Ranjit Pandit

It was an accident that we arrived in Bombay a few days before the monsoon started blowing. One morning, peaceful blue skies and a calm Arabian Sea outside the hotel window. The next, howling winds and rain, lots of it. Because agriculture makes up 23 percent of India's economy, a good monsoon can add several percentage points to India's annual GDP growth. The rural farmers who make up 60 percent of India's labor force welcome it.

But my colleague James Boric, who joined me on the India leg of my trip, and I were not prepared for the rain. We spent the first hour after it started sipping beers and watching the trees sway in the courtyard behind the hotel. The tree roots don't go deep, and they are tall—about 60 to 90 feet.

Even if you got a D in high school physics (like I did), you could see that something had to give. I turned to James and pointed to a tree that was swaying in an especially alarming way. "That tree is going to fall."

"What?"

"That tree. It's going to fall."

I picked up the digital camera on the table. These cameras are so advanced today that you can record short movies on them with the proper memory card. Turning the camera on, I pointed it at the tree and waited.

It took 50 seconds. And then the tree fell. "There it goes," you can hear me say on the video. If only forecasting India's economic future were so easy.

THE NEXT CHINA?

India is the second most populous country in the world, after China. With over 1 billion people, India has its very own economic and social problems: unemployment over 9 percent (the United States is at about 5.5 percent) and annual inflation of 4.6 percent (compared to U.S. inflation at 0.6 percent).

But the most pressing problems are simpler: food and jobs. Bombay alone has 17 million citizens, larger than any U.S. city. Calcutta has 14 million. Even the capital, New Delhi, has 10 million people. Nationally, annual per capita income is only $2,900, far below the poverty level by U.S. standards. The problems are cultural, social, economic, and political. It is difficult to imagine how any central government can meet the needs of such a diverse population—especially a democratically elected government that's actually accountable to so many diverse interests!

Yet India has many obvious advantages over China. The Indian legal system is transparent. The language of business is English. And the workforce is both skilled and highly educated. While the country is 81 percent Hindu, most other world religions are represented as well. It is truly the world's largest and most tolerant and multicultural democracy.

True, the border with Pakistan is a constant hot spot between the Hindu and Muslim worlds. That's especially troubling because both India and Pakistan have nuclear capability. In such a vast and complex country, where the government recognizes more than 1,600 languages and dialects, what are the prospects for India in the twenty-first century? Let's first deal with the risk. Later, we'll look at the opportunities in India's internal market, including its appetite for food.

POLITICAL AND STRATEGIC

There are two major kinds of risk you must be willing to assume if you decide to invest in India: political and strategic. For 60 years, India and Pakistan have been bitter rivals, fighting several times since India's independence in 1947. And although the previous Vajpayee government in India made progress with General Musharraf in Pakistan—by setting up a nuclear hotline and having regular diplomatic discussions—the risk of war (conventional and nuclear) still exists today.

One of the scenarios in the Pentagon's infamous *Asia 2025* report is that Pakistan becomes destabilized by Islamic terrorists. In order to secure Pakistan's nuclear arsenal (according to the scenario in the report), India and the United States might have to conduct a joint conventional strike against Pakistan's military, while special forces would secure the nuclear arsenal.

Unfortunately, I think the nuclear demon is already loose on the black market—no matter what you hear in the U.S. media outlets. And as long as that remains true, the strategic risk of war between India and Pakistan is a real one. And of course, if that happens, owning Indian assets will be perilous.

POLITICAL RISK OR NOT?

The real question on most investors' minds is whether or not the new government represents a threat to India's economic progress. Are politics about to supersede markets in India again?

I'll give you the short answer: No. Here's the longer answer: India is desperately trying to catch up with China. India is just now opening up its economy the way China started to in 1978.

Before that, India operated on a planned economy, with a legendary bureaucracy and layers of red tape that would make the IRS envious. That kind of state interference in the economy is hard to unwind quickly. But as in China, it's the communists who appeared to have learned first how to unleash the productive power of the free market.

For example, the regional government of West Bengal is nominally communist. But West Bengal is a hotbed for outsourcing, so strikes have been banned. The industry cranks out code and phone calls 24/7/365. Local communists at the grassroots level began agitating against the long hours. West Bengal leaders knew that the new business is the key to continued prosperity. They took care of a key malcontent by doing what would please any power-hungry bureaucrat: They promoted him to the national government in New Delhi and kept the phone banks running.

If communists are leading the way in smashing labor laws in order to protect the growth of the outsourcing industry, you can be sure that this current government isn't going to get in the way of it, either—or of any reforms designed to gradually unleash India's economy.

The heart of the issue is whether the current government is going to roll back the privatization efforts of the last government. The answer is that it will slow down the pace of selling state-owned assets. In this sense, India is hardly different from France, which is also currently reluctant to sell off state assets. If slower privatization *is* a risk, it's in the energy sector. But first . . . does India have dollar risk?

FREE FROM THE GREENBACK

The general perception in India is that the country is not totally immune to dollar/interest rate risk, but that it *is* relatively dollar immune. India has far fewer dollar reserves and U.S. Treasury investments than other Asian central banks.

India does have indirect dollar risk. For example, it might be true that a rise in U.S. interest rates isn't going to force India's central bank to raise rates. Indian rates are already significantly higher than in the United States. Indian growth—which is powered mostly by domestic activity—isn't going to be slowed down by higher global rates.

Where India has already been hurt, though, is in the stock market. The "elephant money" (hedge funds that pay attention to interest rate differentials) has already stampeded out of the market, leaving the Bombay exchange with absolutely pathetic volume.

In other words, investors are still treating India as an emerging market. At the first sign of trouble, it's run home to the dollar momma and the U.S. markets, even U.S. bonds. This tells me that with the most mobile global capital, India is still perceived as a speculative play, to be indulged in when interest rates make risk taking relatively cheap. That's bad for the image of India. But it's probably good for you as an investor. And here's why . . .

Despite the apathy in the equity market here, the real economy is indeed growing. Like China five years ago, it needs huge fixed capital investment. The big areas I see are roads, water, rail, electricity, and airports. This is the basic infrastructure of a market economy. It makes the efficient transport of goods and services possible. Without it, you have chaos and inefficiency, which is a pretty good city motto for Bombay. The short story is that India doesn't have the money to pay for infrastructure. It will need foreign direct investment. And to attract that investment, it needs to make tax laws more transparent. Given the large population, low per capita earnings, high unemployment, and relatively high inflation, a lot of economics work against India's move toward true industrialization. Adding to this is the mix of labor, which remains 60 percent agricultural, 23 percent service, and only 17 percent industrial.

India's need for huge, capital-intensive investment would not be supported by local economic forces. You would expect to see a more labor-intensive economy, for example. The need for agricultural labor is a direct factor of India's population mix, but even so, the country is not yet competing—overall—with its economic competitors such as China, central Europe, and the United States. The need to attract outside investment will serve as one of many sources of pressure on higher commodity prices. Even if Chinese consumption of raw materials slows down, India's is just beginning. So commodities are an indirect play on India. But what about a direct play?

GO LOCAL

In the meantime, while the government clears the economic brush, there are many, many Indian companies doing just fine, thank you very much. We have to remember that overall statistics are just that, an averaging of the economy at large. There are several Indian companies that already have cash flow and trade at relatively low multiples to earnings. Some of them do business primarily in the domestic market. Some are exporters. Some are IT and outsourcing firms. Sectors to look at closely: tech services, business services, pharma, and specialty manufacturing industries. A play on government investment would have you looking at telecom, construction, and the auto business.

What they all have in common is that they're being thoroughly ignored right now. But if I'm right that the growth here in India is just picking up, it's the economy that's going to lead the stock market. Now, when the big money is bailing, is the time to find value.

How long will you have to wait? India's fate, like that of much of the region, is tied to the dollar standard. The world is still U.S.-centric. Global capital still flows to America when geopolitical risks increase. Why will that be any different five years from now?

The big difference between today and five years ago is that the current account deficit is much less likely to be financed when U.S. asset markets are underperforming. The whole export-to-America-and-reinvest-the-profits-in-Treasury-securities plan breaks down when interest rates rise and the back of a 20-year bull market in bonds is broken. India's own balance of trade (importing $74 billion per year while exporting $57 billion) feeds the U.S. dollar, as the United States, not surprisingly, remains India's largest trade partner. Even so, we have to be troubled by the prospect of rising interest rates and the end of the bond bull market bubble.

In other words, the whole underlying structure of the global economy—achieve growth through exports to American consumers—is seriously, fatally challenged by falling bond prices.

As Asia begins to unwind its dollar risk, it finds that intra-Asian markets and domestic demand are much healthier ways to achieve noninflationary economic growth, which will be very appealing to the Indian government with its current high inflation rate. That means a rebalancing of currency reserves is in order.

Who will that benefit the most? The euro? Gold? Hard assets? Probably a combination of all three. But after the rebalancing, and what I believe will be another substantial decline in the dollar, the economic fundamentals of a growing India and a mature China will be firmly in place, waiting for investors to view these countries as the new crucial center of the global economic order, and not just peripheral plays for quick returns when interest rates are low.

Of course, if I didn't believe any of that, I wouldn't have spent time traveling through India and looking for the best industries and sectors to own when the world finally sees the domestic growth stories taking place.

It might be true that a rise in U.S. interest rates isn't going to force India's central bank to high rates, which are already significantly higher than in the United States. And that means Indian growth—which is powered mostly by domestic activity—isn't going to be slowed down by higher global rates. The domestic emphasis of India's economy is based partly on need and partly on historical inability to compete globally. Let's not forget the population, political, and economic realities. India *is* emerging as a twenty-first-century player, but as a twentieth-century third-world nation, it has a long way to go.

The big issue, as far as I'm concerned, is whether start-up businesses can get the capital they need. Is risk adequately funded in India? According to various Indian economists and bankers I talked with, good, well-managed projects don't have any trouble raising money in the equity markets. Of course, many of India's major problems won't be funded by the equity markets at all. Physical infrastructure (roads, electric, water, rail, airports) is usually financed through the bond market. Social infrastructure (education, health care, welfare) is usually financed through government spending. On the latter score, the government is already in a tight spot. On the former score, there doesn't seem to be any great rush to structure bond issues to pay for the upgrade in physical infrastructure.

About all that's left is foreign direct investment. India needs a lot more of it. And so the conditions to attract foreign capital (transparent laws and a more efficient tax system for starters) have to be in place before the real upgrades can take place. I'm sure the government knows this, of course (governments are on the ball right?). We'll see what they do to attract more foreign capital.

The good news is that last time India faced a series of exogenous shocks, in 1991, the private sector actually got better at using capital more efficiently. When there's less of it to go around, you husband it and manage it well, or you lose it. The government got out of the "license raj" business, telling business how much to produce. And the market got more competitive. Austrian economist Friedrich Hayek would have loved it. Hayek believed markets work better than governments. Once you free up prices to communicate information on quality, prices tend to go down and services tend to improve. In any event, Indian business appears to be better at using capital. Which leads to the obvious question: *Just which businesses are we talking about here?*

THE END OF THE LICENSE RAJ

Ranjit Pandit is a managing director for the Indian office of McKinsey & Company. McKinsey does management consulting globally. Being a macro, top-down guy myself, there's no better way to start your evaluation of a country than by getting the lay of the investment and economic land from someone who knows. So that's what I did.

Over pumpkin tea and two hours of conversation, two issues jumped out at me as being critical to your attention if you're forming an India strategy. The first is obvious, the second less so.

I'll begin with the obvious issue on U.S. investor's minds: outsourcing. I came to India as an outsourcing skeptic. That is, my initial impression was that it's a far bigger issue in the press than it is in the economy, or for investors. Having been there, I've revised that opinion.

Outsourcing *is* a big industry in India.

India has a well-educated, mostly English-speaking population willing to work at a discount to Western labor costs. But Mr. Pandit said multinational firms like British Airways are finding that their

Indian workers are also able to deliver substantial cost savings over and above the cost of labor. The airline industry offers an example in the efficiency of code-share tickets. BA pays a fee to other airlines when you buy a ticket through BA but take part of your journey on a different carrier. The problem for BA is that, prior to outsourcing, it wasn't managing those claims efficiently, verifying whether it was overpaying, not to mention the labor hours spent in actually processing the claims (or reimbursing the other carrier). Mr. Pandit said BA was able to compound its outsourcing cost savings through the additional efforts of its Indian employees to actually run the operation more efficiently.

This is an obvious benefit to shareholders in multinational firms that are using outsourcing to handle larger and larger portions of their business services. It's not just labor cost, in other words, but additional benefits. That's the value of having an educated workforce on the other end of the service contract.

Mr. Pandit figures that 20 percent of all Western services could be headed to the Indian outsourcing market. That makes it a major industry in India, and probably an investable theme if you can find the right outsourcing firms. As a skeptic, I objected that outsourcing might have diminished domestic benefit because the profits of the firms were going to multinationals, not Indian firms. Perhaps, came the answer. But even if the benefit were just the wages and taxes being paid by multinationals, it would be well worth it for India to develop the industry along its current trajectory. As part of an effort to at least equalize the economy between service and agricultural, it demonstrates a larger global trend. What remains is India's lagging industry (only 17 percent of the workforce). Perhaps India is destined to become the new global service sector.

I won't say I'm sold on *all* aspects of the outsourcing question. I think that, as a political issue, outsourcing is overdone. Americans tend to look at it purely as an issue of American jobs and, in reality, America insources far more jobs than it outsources—so the heated arguments about "unAmerican" business practices are overblown.

I agree with Mr. Pandit that political concerns won't stop the trend if it makes sense for business. And if he's right, it *does* make sense for business—both Indian business and international business. This sounds counterintuitive if you look at the headlines and listen to the trends. The *real* trends, I mean. "Nothing in India is as it appears," Mr. Pandit said.

UNLEASHING DOMESTIC DEMAND

Retail is one of the few industries yet to be deregulated, largely on the strength of the trade lobby, which makes a killing on the myriad taxes imposed on retail trade. A value-added tax (VAT) streamlines the revenue collection for the government but eats into the margins of retailers, hence the strenuous objections. No one likes their revenue model changed for the worse.

If a VAT is passed and foreign direct investment in India's retail sector becomes a reality (it's not right now), you'd have that Holy Grail of balanced economies—domestic demand and export growth working hand in hand to raise living standards.

There are dozens of examples of how the current retail trade regime suppresses domestic demand and leaves savings sitting in banks. And truthfully, the frugal miser in me wonders if you really want to unleash consumer culture in a country with a high savings rate.

But the law shouldn't prevent people from spending money if they want to. After all, it *is* money, not credit, which is much less of a problem here, by all appearances. Unleashed domestic demand with a VAT increases the tax base, promotes the growth of domestic industry, and lets people buy what they want without being punished by high taxes or higher prices than they might otherwise pay.

Funny that this idea should come up so soon after the death of Ronald Reagan. It looks a lot like a *Laffer curve*—that by reducing nominal tax rates (or indirect retail taxes) you increase spending and productivity, which broadens the tax base, leading to increased government revenue and more consumer choice at lower prices. It's Reagan's nirvana.

Maybe it is, indeed, just gringopomorphic for me to think of India's growth in Reaganesque terms. But chuck out Reagan and you still find that the difference between Chinese and Indian GDP per capita growth rates over the last five years (and probably since

1978, when the door in China flew open) is the importance of domestic demand to overall economic growth.

THE COMING BOOM?

On my trip, I spent time in Bombay and found it to be rainy, colorful, pungent, and humid. Add to that the 17 million people, and you have the picture. India is styling itself as the China of the next five years, an emerging giant that's just beginning to hit its investment stride.

India, like China, faces an enormous *rural agrarian* population—60 percent of the labor force—that's failed to enjoy the benefits of the country's recent prosperity. This means that now is a pretty good time to be on the ground in India to find out just where things stand. Is it the next China? Is it even better? Or do the facts support the investment hype?

My first impression, after driving the hour from the airport to the Taj Mahal Hotel on the water, is that India, like China, will probably see a huge boom in fixed capital investment. Its comparative advantage in low-cost service jobs is well documented. But like any emerging market, it needs more physical infrastructure, not least to support such a large population. I'm talking about roads, water treatment plants, and rural electrification.

These are basic needs for a large economy, much as in China. It's not a bad idea to keep things simple when you're first investing in an overseas market. When you're looking at the Asian story as an investor, it's easy to get lost in the big ideas. There are a lot of them. When will China float the yuan? Has Japan turned the corner? What will happen to commodity prices now that 4 billion more people are competing for the same scarce natural resources?

Then there are urgent economic questions. When will Asian central banks change their macroeconomic and exchange rate policies? Will Asian governments shift policies away from encouraging exporters and toward more balanced economic growth and stronger local currencies? Will higher oil prices and interest rates put the brakes on economic growth all over the world?

Where are the good businesses at good values?

You ask yourself the same questions buying stocks in Asia as you'd ask yourself in America. How does the company make money? How does it make more money than that? How much do you have to pay for this year's earnings? Does the business make sense to you?

Smarter investors than I will make money finding little-known technology and manufacturing companies in Asia. Those stories are sexier. The potential payouts are enormous. So are the risks and earnings multiples.

I prefer to focus on businesses satisfying a known demand with a profitable product. The more I look at Asian stocks or the stocks of Western firms doing business in Asia, the clearer it becomes that it doesn't make sense to take more risk than you have to. There are a lot of risks, of course. But you know that already. I mention it now simply to remind you that 70 percent of your total return on any investment comes from being in the right asset class. In other words, you can own the best company in the world, but if stocks are in a bear market, you're in the wrong asset class.

If you buy stocks today, you're counting on some combination of the following three forces being in your favor (and staying that way):

1. You're counting on commodities being in a long-term (secular) bull market that supports food prices.

2. You're counting on the fundamental shift in global economic fortunes from the West to the East (the money migration).

3. You're counting on the debt-burdened U.S. dollar leading to an inevitable global currency realignment: the world getting off the dollar standard and Asian central banks dumping their trillions' worth of dollar assets.

Each of these three forces suggests a powerful driver behind higher prices for certain stocks. It won't be a straight line up to overnight profits. In fact, China and all of Asia are entering a cycle of minibooms and minibusts. The important fact to note is that the overall trend is up. (I don't buy for one minute this business about a "soft landing" in China.) Asia today is similar to the United States in the nineteenth century. It's a volatile place with a wildcat mentality. Back then, all of North America was industrializing, modernizing, and fantasizing about a richer future. Now it's Asia's turn.

Some of the best investments at the beginning of America's century of global dominance were in downright modest companies—Levi Strauss selling workmen's clothes to the prospectors of the California gold rush is the best example. It didn't matter to Strauss if fortune hunters in California struck gold. He had already struck it outfitting them all. Or take electricity. Think of the appliances in your house that use it. Each of those is a business, a product, a stock. But they all come back to electricity. Without it, all of them are useless.

Now think of Asia in the same terms. A million fortunes will be made. Thousands of new businesses will be created. It's happening in China as we speak. But regardless of the business, the fundamental economic demands of human beings are not going to change, and that in itself is the basis of a powerful and relatively safe investment idea: Invest in the businesses that directly feed the growing trends.

MORE MOUTHS TO FEED AND PROFITS TO BE MADE

The populations of the world's poorest countries are set to grow by 55 percent in the next 50 years, according to the Population Reference Bureau (PRB).[1] India will pass China as the world's biggest country. There will be 3 billion more mouths to feed all over the globe.

What may save the day for us is that some of the world's richest countries are actually getting smaller. Chalk it up to religion, atheism, birth control, or just selfish living, but a lot of countries are going to be less populous. For example, according to the PRB, Bulgaria will contract about 40 percent, from a current population of 7.8 million to 4.8 million, by 2050.

Southern European countries, including Italy, Portugal, and Greece, are expected to lose at least 10 percent of their current populations. Worst of all is Japan. The PRB report claims that in Japan "only 14 percent of the population is below age 15, while 19 percent is above age 65."[2] Based on these numbers, the Japanese population will contract by 21 percent over the next 50 years.

Yet despite smaller populations in Europe and Japan, world population is growing. That means more people competing for the same scarce resources. And when it comes to food, those resources are already stretched thin.

The U.S. Department of Agriculture publishes a painfully dry monthly report called *World Agricultural Supply and Demand Estimates* (WASDE). Here are some highlights from a recent report:

- *Price pressures build:* 2004's wheat crop of 609 million tons was the second largest on record. But wheat stocks, the surplus amount of wheat in storage, are actually at 30-year lows. The report says price pressures will soon start building, because wheat stocks have not been dramatically rebuilt.

- *Grain consumption exceeds production:* In all of the last four years, world grain production has fallen short of consumption, forcing a drawdown of stocks in wheat, corn, rice, and soybeans. Soybean prices recently hit 15-year highs, and wheat and corn 7-year highs.

- *Reserves being drawn down:* Despite the largest U.S. corn crop in history projected, the WASDE report said that the global stocks-to-use ratio for corn will be at a 30-year low, with stocks drawing down for the fifth straight year.

These numbers aren't just bad news; quite the contrary. I don't believe we're headed for a Malthusian famine. What these statistics show me, coupled with what I saw on the ground everywhere in Asia, is that there is a tremendous opportunity for food growers. But which growers? Should you buy at the wholesale or the retail level? And aren't rising commodity prices bad for companies that sell food products? Well—yes. Think of oil refiners. A refiner makes gasoline and other products from oil. When the price of oil goes up, the refiner has to pay more for the chief input of its product. Oil is a cost for refiners. Higher oil prices squeeze margins. True, if oil prices are high, it means gasoline prices are probably high, too. But we live in a competitive world. Producers are not always able to pass on the higher cost of raw materials directly to consumers. Raise your price and your customers may decide to get their gasoline from that station across the street.

The good news is that we may be seeing the peak of commodity prices in the short term. This will mean a big boost in the profit margins of the companies that are well positioned to profit from this trend. And you can buy these companies today before that boost is priced in to the stocks.

Long term, though, based on the population statistics I mentioned, the demand for basic food commodities is one of the bedrock economic truths of our lifetimes. Food is in growing demand, and supply is increasingly tight. You don't have to be an economist to understand a story like this. And you don't even have to be from a big family, as I am, where opening your mouth to speak at the dinner table means you have less time to shove in mashed potatoes before they disappear.

The argument for food (and for a select few other raw commodity companies) is basic common sense. It's an investment theme that's easy to understand and hard to argue with. And not only are the numbers behind you on this trend, but the returns on your investment over the next five years will be as good as anything else you can get in the world.

FILLING GLOBAL BELLIES

Don't be surprised if you haven't heard that China is tightening rules on soybean oil imports. It's not exactly making headlines. But that's okay. It means very few investors are looking at the investment opportunity in food, agriculture, and raw materials.

There's an old saying in China that the Chinese will eat anything under the sky with four legs, except the table and the chair. And you wouldn't have to go far from a Chinese dinner table—or any dinner table in Asia for that matter—to see the moneymaking opportunity from Asia's gaping appetite. If you knew what you were looking for, that is.

What you're looking for is cooking oil. Soybean oil especially. Cooking oil is used in woks all over China—and all over the world, to be fair. Soybeans are key to the food product. China imported 6.26 million tons of soybeans in the first five months of 2004, or about $2.25 billion worth. That already exceeded the total amount for 2003.

Those numbers don't include soybean oil imports. In the first half of 2004, China imported 1.4 million metric tons of soybean oil at a price of U.S. $850 million. That's also double 2003's consumption. In fact, China is the world's largest importer of soybeans and soybean oil.

COMPETE GLOBALLY, FEED LOCALLY

Chinese soybean dependency is getting so large, in fact, that the government has raised requirements on soybean import quality in a bid to favor the domestic industry. By the way, this is just one part of what I see as an overall strategy by China to build institutions that make China less dependent on foreign commodities in financial markets.

Where you see it most is in the sprouting up of commodity exchanges in Dalian (near North Korea), Zhenzhou, and Shanghai. The Chinese are trying to provide domestic producers with cheaper ways to sell production forward and hedge future price risk. It's all an attempt to make sure Chinese agriculture and industry can compete globally and feed locally.

The targets of these new regulations are Argentina and Brazil. Brazilian soybean exports to China went up fourfold from 2003 to 2004, to over 419,000 tons. Argentina's doubled to over 950,000 tons. With soybean prices at 15-year highs and Chinese demand at record levels, it's easy to see why the government is concerned. It's also easy to see why soybeans and soybean oil are our first Asia/China investment opportunity.

SUPERMARKET TO THE FAR EAST

With all due respect to Archer Daniels Midland, Latin America is rapidly turning into the supermarket of Asia. The heartthrob of the global left, Luiz Inácio Lula da Silva, was in China while I visited. Lula!, as he's popularly known, has been president of Brazil since 2002. And he was in China to cement bilateral ties between China and the world's emerging food and iron ore powers.

It's not just Brazil. The Chinese have quietly gone about locking up bilateral agreements with some of the most natural resource–laden countries in the world: a deal with New Zealand, which for years has been a veritable farm of high-value agricultural goods to Australia and England; a deal with Malaysia in late May, with a concentration on agriculture, resource, and infrastructure ties; and a deal with Argentina in late June of this year for investment and agriculture ties between the two countries.

Notice a pattern here? Without relying on unfriendly geopolitical rivals like the United States, China has gone throughout Asia and to politically neutral countries in Latin America to secure access to the raw materials (food, metals, energy) that it knows it will need to power its economy ahead in the twenty-first century. China is even on course to conclude a free trade agreement with Australia sometime in 2005 that will give it still more access to the rich natural resource wealth of Australia.

THE BEST STOCK TO FEED ASIA

To invest in the China/soybean/Latin America story, I recommend you look at companies like Bunge (BG). Bunge is engaged in an easy-to-understand business: It helps feed the world and makes a profit doing it. According to the company's own description: Bunge is a global agribusiness and food company with integrated operations that stretch from the farm field to the retail shelf and circle the globe. We capture value wherever it appears on the food production chain by

- Producing and selling fertilizer to farmers
- Buying, handling, and selling oilseeds and grains
- Crushing oilseeds to make meal and oil for the livestock and food processing industries
- Producing edible oils and related products for food service customers and consumers

Bunge is the world's largest oilseed processing company. It's the largest producer and supplier of fertilizers to farmers in South America. And it's the world's leading seller of bottled vegetable oil to consumers. From raw materials to finished product, Bunge has a strong position in its market.

In Argentina, Bunge is the country's largest soy processor. It's also the largest wheat producer and fertilizer manufacturer in the country. It's the second largest agricultural exporter in the country and the third largest exporter, period. I didn't set out, by the way, looking for a proxy on the Argentine commodity sector. But Bunge appears to be a good one.

What's Bunge's connection with the Chinese market, you're wondering? The company doesn't make its export market numbers available on a line-item basis. It does point out, however, that per capita consumption of soybeans in China has grown at 4 percent a year since 1994 and that vegetable oil consumption has grown at twice that rate.

Bunge is not strictly a China play. It's an international company with a footprint all over the globe. In the United States it has customers in the food processing industry that include baked goods companies like General Mills, Inc., McKee Foods Corporation, and Sara Lee Corporation. Its Brazilian food processing customers include Nestlé, Groupe Danone, and Nabisco. In also has food service customers in the United States, including Sysco Corporation, Ruby Tuesday, Inc., Krispy Kreme Doughnuts Inc., and Yum! Brands, Inc. And even in Brazil, Bunge is a major supplier of frying and baking shortening to McDonald's Corporation. It has European clients like Unilever and Nestlé.

Anytime you buy a stock, you take a risk. But if you're looking for a strong stock to capitalize on a fundamental economic demand—food, both the growing of it and the processing and selling of it—Bunge is the ticket.

There are a lot of other tickets, too, and a lot of other rides you could take all over the world. It's time to step back again and look at the best investments driving growth, not just in India and China but all over the planet—even in America.

Before I left Bombay, I had dinner with a *Strategic Investment* reader, Pinank Mehta, and his wife. Pinank himself was skeptical of India's prospects. He knows that you can fake economic growth by spending a lot of money and creating a lot of economic activity. It's not the same thing as creating wealth. That takes time. It also takes institutions that treat money well. India is still working on those. Most of its lending is still done through the banking system. And like China, it finds itself on the horns of a dilemma: how to lead the twenty-first-century without leaving behind the hundreds of millions of rural farmers who have yet to enjoy any of the benefits of the growing prosperity of Asia's two titans.

They were all good questions. Pinank realized the ride won't be easy and that a bust in U.S. stocks will hurt India more than she expects. He's a contrarian's contrarian. How do I know for sure? We went to the best Chinese restaurant in Bombay.

CHAPTER 8

INSIDE THE DECISION CYCLE: THREE FINAL STRATEGIES FOR INVESTING IN TOMORROW'S STOCK MARKET

Our strategic directives were dynamism, initiative, mobility, and rapidity of decision in the face of new situations.

—General Vo Nguyen Giap

Dr. Chet Richards crossed my path at just the right time. About two weeks before I flew from Baltimore to Hong Kong, I spent an hour on the phone discussing his book *Certain to Win* (Xlibris, 2004), which is about what kind of businesses will survive in the intensely competitive world of 2005 and beyond.

Richards is a retired colonel in the U.S. Air Force Reserve. During his career he worked with one of the most important strategic thinkers you probably have never heard of—the late Colonel John Boyd. Among other things, Boyd wrote the manual for air-to-air combat that the military still uses today. He was also a key player in the military reform movement of the late 1970s and early 1980s that led to the use of planes like the A-10 Warthog and the F-16.

However, in his book, Richards has brought Boyd's most important contribution to the public: the Boyd Cycle, or OODA loops.

OODA stands for Observe, Orient, Decide, Act. When Boyd first developed it, his cycle was a description of the decision-making process that led to faster, better decisions in combat. Unbeknownst to many, then defense secretary Dick Cheney called Boyd in when he was drawing up the now-famous battle plan for the first gulf war.

The more recent Iraq war owes many of its characteristics to Boyd's strategic thought as well. The high tempo of operations, the misdirection, and the simultaneous operations in many places at once are all designed to dictate the pace of events and bewilder the enemy. You force them to react to you, but because you're operating at a much faster pace, they're reacting too late, always one step behind. You're inside the enemy's decision cycle. Eventually, the enemy's will to resist collapses.

Richards has taken Boyd's strategic thinking and applied it to business. I was interested in talking to him to see if it also applied to investing. Can the Boyd Cycle teach you how to observe a complicated and fast-moving world of events, orient yourself to its predominant trends, decide the most effective course of action, and then take it quickly?

I think the answer is yes. Think about what we've done up to now. We've observed some of the big trends in the geopolitical and investment worlds, including the dollar crisis in America, the rise of China, and the emergence of new tools to help investors cope. We've oriented ourselves to the changing situation by going to the center of change—Asia—and finding out which trends look promising and which ones are dangerous. Along the way, we've decided to focus on one kind of tool, exchange-traded funds, and decided to concentrate on the simplest, easiest-to-understand trends driving the world's markets. We haven't excluded finding good single stocks to profit, either. And we've found some of those, too!

What about acting? That will be up to you. But before you get to that, let's look at three more opportunities. First, a simple way to invest in emerging markets. Second, more ways to invest in the world's soaring demand for raw materials and food. Finally, coming full circle, we'll examine some trends in America's own economy that look promising for investors.

EMERGING MARKET ETFs

The world moves more quickly now than ever before—making it harder to find profitable investments at the right time. There's always a bull market somewhere; there's always a strongest asset class out there. And no matter where you're investing—or what you're investing in—you still need to get there first to reap the biggest gains. You also need to pick the right stock, and that's where the ETFs come in.

Which of these fledgling markets will emerge triumphant? It's too soon to tell. But you can still successfully participate in these potentially explosive markets while minimizing your risk (and your cost) by investing in a basket of top emerging-market stocks, rather than trying to be right about just one or two. One way to do so is with the iShares MSCI Emerging Markets Index Fund (EEM).

This relatively new ETF (it was launched in April 2003) has already gained tremendously: Since June 19, 2003, it gained 47 percent in 10 months, by April 6, 2004. I expect the fund will continue to grow, since the global factors responsible for its strong start still exist.

Emerging markets benefit when the flow of world capital changes course. And so do specific asset classes, like commodities, as investor confidence dwindles and the thirst for tangibles grows. The commodities market as a whole has seen tremendous growth in recent years, thanks in part to the falling U.S. dollar and insatiable Chinese demand. But the upward trend in these real assets is far from over.

The big guns in the commodities world right now, gold and oil, have been getting an awful lot of press. Gold prices remain strong as the dollar continues to weaken—and gold is the natural choice for nervous investors while equity markets are stuck in limbo. And with continuing tumult in the land of oil at a time of growing demand, we could see even higher crude prices in the near future.

But the world of commodities is populated by other assets as well—steel, timber, aluminum—that make up the very backbone of the manufacturing trade. Although many of these vital necessities come from countries in what seems like continual upheaval, many of them are produced in one of the most stable economies in the world: Australia.

Australia, secure in its position as one of the world's strongest commodity producers, is primed to profit substantially from this bull market. With proximity to China, Australia can easily position itself as the major exporter of raw materials needed to fuel the Asian boom. In fact, I like Australia so much I'm moving there! The quality of life is outstanding. And it's part of the greatest investment story of our lifetimes. But you don't have to move to Australia to invest in emerging global bull markets.

Let's take a closer look at EEM. To find out what EEM owns, you can check at www.ishares.com. EEM is designed to track the performance of the Morgan Stanley Capital International (MSCI) Emerging Markets Index. To give you an idea of the composition of that index, consider the top 10 country weights. EEM is weighted by sector. And by the way, this kind of transparency—knowing exactly what you own each and every month—is a big difference between traditional mutual funds and exchange-traded funds. The more you know about what you own, the better the risk assessments you can make.

Top 10 Country Weights, MSCI Emerging Markets Index

South Korea	16.29%
South Africa	16.26%
Taiwan	9.06%
Brazil	8.03%
China	8.53%
Mexico	7.27%
India	5.70%
Russia	4.58%
Israel	4.49%
Thailand	3.58%

Korea, by the way, is a good example of the risk you take when buying an emerging market. Sometimes it *is* better to buy the best stock, like KEPCO (Korea Electric Power). It depends on the situation. As you can see from Figure 8.1, EWK (the Korea ETF) did well in 2004, making a new all-time high.

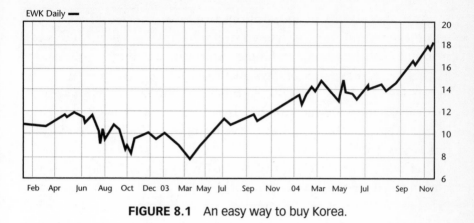

FIGURE 8.1 An easy way to buy Korea.

Things weren't always that rosy. From January 2002 until March 2003, EWK was both thinly traded and getting clobbered—losing nearly 40 percent from May 2002 to March 2003. It's a good correlation with what happened on South Korea's KOSPI Index during the same time. Check Figure 8.2. I point *that* out because I believe we're in a transition phase in global markets—another clue pointing you in the direction of becoming a bull hunter.

It's a good thing to see so much cash come off the sidelines and into emerging market funds (especially ones *you* own). But keep in mind that what the "hot money" giveth, it often taketh away. Hedge funds view emerging markets, generally speaking, as speculations or interest rate trades. With rates moving up in the United States, the hedge fund money and institutional money that went trolling for higher capital gains in emerging markets (with lots of leverage, thanks to low interest rates) can suddenly reverse and come home to the Dow. That means an emerging market can become a submerging market in the blink of an eye—as when India's SET index lost 17 percent in a few days.

A support for emerging markets going forward is the growing belief that a falling dollar and continued U.S. deficits are reducing the demand for U.S. financial assets, both government bonds and U.S. stocks. This transition—out of American financial assets and into

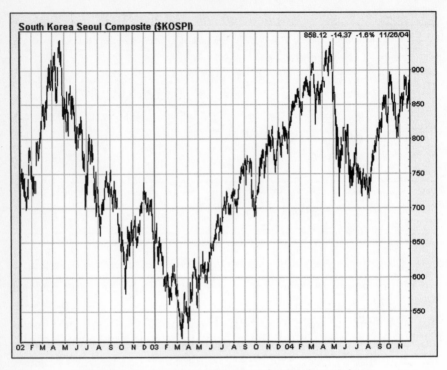

FIGURE 8.2 The ups and downs of emerging markets.
(Source: © 2004 DecisionPoint.com)

foreign stocks and bonds—is one part of the money migration (labor and capital being two others).

That doesn't mean you won't see some hesitation on the part of investors. The move into emerging markets is fashionable, but is it durable? That's what you need to watch for. For example, if you own EEM, be prepared for a correction. EEM, after all, is a stock. And like every other stock, there's risk to owning it.

Even so, I still like the holdings in EEM. There were 27 companies that make up more than 1 percent of EEM's net assets at the end of 2004. Some of the big names in EEM include Samsung Electronics (6.45 percent), Anglo American PLC (3.35 percent), Posco (2.72 percent), Taiwan Semiconductor (2.70 percent), Lukoil (2.06 percent), Korea Electric Power (2.03 percent), Infosys (1.73 percent), Surgetneftegaz (1.68 percent), China Mobile (1.55 percent), Petroleo Brasileiro (1.54 percent), Teva Pharmaceutical Industries (1.42 percent),

Telefonos de Mexico (1.44 percent), Sasol (1.28 percent), SK Telecom (1.21 percent), PetroChina (1.26 percent), and Companhia Vale do Rio Doce (1.21 percent).

By the way, you see in this list something worth taking note of in emerging markets. The largest, most liquid stocks tend to be telecoms, power/energy/utility companies, and natural resource companies, depending on the country's native real assets (coal, oil, or natural gas, for example).

THE RULE-OF-THREE STRATEGY FOR EMERGING MARKETS

As a bull hunter, you need to work from tried-and-true guidelines that are effective. Be aware of a crude but simple *rule of three* when looking at any one particular emerging market. Find the biggest telecom, the biggest financial, and the biggest oil/energy/resource company. When you've found them, you've probably found three of the largest, most liquidly traded stocks in the country. And they'll probably have foreign listings, giving you an even safer way to buy them.

One quick look at the industry and sector composition of EEM in Table 8.1 confirms the importance of finding the basic strengths in

TABLE 8.1 TOP SECTORS/INDUSTRIES (AS OF 10/31/2004)

1. Materials	16.08%
2. Telecommunication services	14.71%
3. Energy	13.30%
4. Banks	12.76%
5. Semiconductors and semiconductor equipment	12.58%
6. Utilities	4.22%
7. Software and services	3.66%
8. Food, beverage and tobacco	2.63%
9. Insurance	2.37%
10. Pharmaceuticals and biotechnology	2.27%

Source: iShares.com

emerging market economies and investing in those—while leaving the out-and-out speculation to the speculators. Resources, telecom, energy, and financials are the big sectors. You have some risk, especially with the banks and the semiconductor companies. But you manage that risk through broad diversification—both geographically and via sectors—and the entire portfolio is poised to benefit as money and interest focus on economies outside the United States.

STERNER STUFF TO PROFIT FROM

In the last two chapters, we looked at satisfying China's and Asia's demand for food. But it's hard to ignore the iron ore business or Companhia Vale do Rio Doce (CVRD for short, but ticker symbol RIO). The company reported record profits of $535 million in the second quarter of 2004. It's what you'd expect from the world's largest miner and exporter of iron ore at a time when the world's demand for iron ore is booming.

CVRD has been especially adept at taking advantage of booming Chinese demand to cement long-term relationships with international clients and even develop mining operations overseas. CVRD signed a framework agreement to build a $1 billion alumina refinery in northeastern Brazil with the Aluminum Corporation of China Ltd. (ACH), or Chalco, the largest alumina and aluminum producer in China. It's a huge deal.

Chalco joins a host of global aluminum titans trying to stake claims to South American and Caribbean bauxite deposits, as limited supplies and strong demand boost prices along the aluminum product chain. Bauxite is used to make alumina, a white powder that is then used to make primary aluminum. Relatively low energy costs make Latin America an attractive place to operate.

For CVRD, the Chalco agreement means it finally has the guaranteed client it needs to further develop its aluminum business, part of a long-term goal to diversify its mining base. The company's aluminum business currently accounts for just under 15 percent of revenue compared with more than 70 percent for iron. In short, the iron ore business has been great and promises to stay that way. But the company is planning other ways to bring in more revenue. And the Chinese like what they're seeing from Latin American companies like RIO, despite the comparatively high cost of shipping.

Shipping ore from Brazil to China is far more costly than shipping from some other big mineral producers such as Australia. However, the idea of producing intermediary products locally—refining bauxite to alumina and iron ore to steel slabs—seems to be extremely appealing to Chinese companies. Brazil's richest iron ore and bauxite deposits are located on the edge of the Amazon near the state of Para, just a train ride from ports along the northeastern coast. Those ports, in turn, are just a few days by boat from the Panama Canal. China, for its part, has shown an eagerness to seal up accords with anyone who has the real assets in the ground that China needs.

THE DOLLAR AND FOREIGN TRADE

Everyone knows and says that America's twin deficits must fall for the dollar to stabilize. But which deficit is more likely to actually come down? And will it actually arrest the dollar's fall? Every bull hunter should be interested in the answers to these questions; no matter what the outcome, there will be opportunities.

We know that American manufactured goods can't compete in terms of price with Chinese manufactured goods, at least in industries where the Chinese are engaged in competition, due to the huge disparity in labor costs (not even getting into currency values). In aerospace, American goods are competitive because the Chinese are not involved in aerospace . . . yet. It's an industry that requires high-skilled labor. It's capital-intensive and requires complicated, specialized machine tools.

Yet despite these advantages, the trade deficit soars, month after month (see Figure 8.3). In order to profit from it, we'll have to look deeper at just what kind of American firms are doing well already and compete in the twenty-first century.

The Department of Commerce's Bureau of Economic Analysis (BEA) breaks down trade in goods into six categories. If we want to know where the deficit in goods is coming from, and whether or not

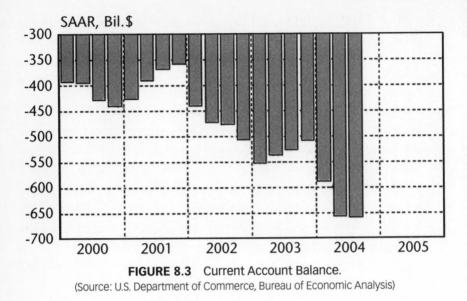

FIGURE 8.3 Current Account Balance.
(Source: U.S. Department of Commerce, Bureau of Economic Analysis)

it can be reduced by a falling dollar, we need to know how it's composed. The six categories are

1. Food, feed, and beverages
2. Industrial supplies (which includes petroleum and petroleum products)
3. Capital goods
4. Automotive vehicles
5. Consumer goods
6. Other

To find out where the deficit is coming from we need to look at both exports and imports. Specifically, where, if anywhere, is the United States generating surpluses (or at least where is it in the neighborhood of being competitive)? And where, on the other hand, are the largest deficits? How might those deficits be corrected?

It's also important to keep in mind where most of the trade is taking place. That is, the United States may be competitive in food, feed, and beverages, but that category may hold such a small percentage of total trade that it's unlikely a large surplus on small volume would have any material effect on the overall deficit. That doesn't mean, however, that it isn't a clue for investors about where you might find individual companies that *will* do well on a falling dollar. Let's look at exports first.

BONA FIDE CAPITAL GOODS SELLERS

Things haven't been all bad for U.S. exporters—even for exporters of goods and manufactured items. In the first nine months of 2004, U.S. goods exports totaled $597 billion. That was a 13.5 percent increase from the same period in 2003. And even better news was the prominent role of capital goods. Take a look at Tables 8.2 and 8.3. Capital goods dominated in 2003 . . . and again in 2004.

As you can see, the two big players in terms of exports were capital goods and industrial supplies. Not bad for the so-called new economy, is it? And when you compare the two periods, there was growth across the board in each export category. See Table 8.4.

All right, bull hunters, it's a rosy picture so far. But we've yet to look at the import side of the ledger. And as you already know, these numbers are much larger. They have to be, or there would be no deficit. But a closer look will tell us in which categories the deficit is

TABLE 8.2   WHAT AMERICA EXPORTED
TO THE WORLD IN 2003 . . .

Category	Dollar Volume (in Billions)	% of Total Export Volume
Capital goods	$215.59	40.9%
Industrial supplies	$128.64	24.4%
Consumer goods	$66.49	12.6%
Automotive vehicles	$60.07	11.4%
Food, feed, and beverages	$40.33	7.6%

Export figures from 2003, January–September.
Source: U.S. Department of Commerce, Bureau of Economic Analysis

TABLE 8.3   CAPITAL GOODS SOARED IN 2004, TOO

Category	Dollar Volume (in Billions)	% of Total Export Volume
Capital goods	$246.59	41%
Industrial supplies	$149.34	24%
Consumer goods	$75.70	12%
Automotive vehicles	$65.37	11%
Food, feed, and beverages	$41.59	6.9%

Source: U.S. Department of Commerce, Bureau of Economic Analysis

being racked up. And later, we'll look at just where American industry *may* be competitive with a much larger drop in the dollar. But first, we take a look at the import numbers.

WHAT AMERICANS ARE BUYING

You already know that Americans spend more than they earn and consume more than they produce. But what are they consuming in such gargantuan quantities? On the goods side of the trade question, the general categories are the same (consumer goods, capital goods, autos, for example). The data in Tables 8.5 and 8.6 show that the same general trends dominated in 2003 and 2004: large total import volumes across the board. Later, I'll compare the import and export volumes to see where the largest deficits lay on a categorical basis.

TABLE 8.4   UNEXPECTED GROWTH IN GOODS EXPORTS

Export Category	% Increase in Export Volumes
Capital goods	14.3%
Industrial supplies	16%
Consumer goods	13.8%
Automotive vehicles	8.8%
Food, feed, and beverages	3.1%

Source: U.S. Department of Commerce, Bureau of Economic Analysis

TABLE 8.5   U.S. GOODS TRADE IMPORT VOLUMES, 2003

Category	Dollar Volume (in Billions)	% of Total Import Volume
Consumer goods	$257	26%
Industrial supplies	$233	24%
Capital goods	$218	23%
Automotive vehicles	$155	16%
Food, feed, and beverages	$41	4.4%

Source: U.S. Department of Commerce, Bureau of Economic Analysis

Tables 8.5 and 8.6 show the same two time series: the first nine months of 2003 versus the first nine months of 2004.

Import volumes, in percentage terms and by category, did not differ much between the first nine months of 2004 and the first nine months of 2003. Industrial supplies (which includes oil) jumped three percentage points to replace consumer goods as the leading category. But overall, the percentages remained the same.

What changed were the dollar volumes. Export volumes grew in 2003. But so did import volumes, albeit at a faster rate. In the first nine months of 2003, imports tallied up at $934 billion. For 2004, the same period saw imports over $1 trillion. They grew at a 15.5 percent clip—two full percentage points faster than exports. And all this while the dollar was weakening.

TABLE 8.6   U.S. GOODS TRADE IMPORT VOLUMES, 2004

Category	Dollar Volume (in Billions)	% of Total Import Volume
Industrial supplies	$295	27%
Consumer goods	$274	25%
Capital goods	$253	23%
Automotive vehicles	$170	15.7%
Food, feed, and beverages	$45.8	4%

Source: U.S. Department of Commerce, Bureau of Economic Analysis

TABLE 8.7   AMERICA'S APPETITE KEEPS ON GROWING

Import Category	% Increase in Import Volumes
Industrial supplies	26%
Capital goods	16%
Food, feed, and beverages	11.2%
Consumer goods	11%
Automotive vehicles	9.4%

Source: U.S. Department of Commerce, Bureau of Economic Analysis

When you break down the import growth on a nine-months-over-nine-months basis, you see that oil imports surged, along with capital goods and consumer goods. See Table 8.7.

Import and export figures for the first nine months of 2004 can be compared by category to see where the U.S. goods deficit is *really* coming from. We know that the goods deficit was $481 billion. But which category was the chief culprit? Table 8.8 shows the answer.

The chart tells the story. But what's the story? There are a couple of conclusions to reach from the number crunching. And they point us in the right direction for our next line of inquiry.

Consumer goods made up 41 percent of the deficit through nine months of 2004. Industrial supplies made up 30 percent and automotive vehicles were 30 percent; capital goods, 1 percent; and food, feed, and beverages, less than 1 percent. The largest deficit was right

TABLE 8.8   THE CONSUMER GOODS DEFICIT GORILLA

Category	Imports Minus Exports (Billions for First 9 Months 2004)	Deficit for Category (Billions)
Consumer goods	$274.3–$75.7	–$198.6
Industrial supplies	$295.5–$149.3	–$146.3
Automotive vehicles	$170.4–$65.3	–$105.0
Capital goods	$253.1–$246.5	–$6.5
Food, feed, and beverages	$45.86–$41.59	–$4.2

Source: U.S. Department of Commerce, Bureau of Economic Analysis

where you'd expect, in consumer goods. But it's not the largest category in terms of total trade volume. Going forward, a reduction in the deficit for consumer goods will mean a reduction in U.S. consumption, fewer imports, and probably not greater exports.

The deficit in food, feed, and beverages is small, but so is the total trade volume ($86 billion), relatively speaking. The United States may have a genuine advantage here that may translate to an actual trade surplus in the future. But because this category is such a small percentage of goods trading volume, it's not enough to throw the overall goods deficit into surplus status. Yet there may still be good companies in the category that merit investor attention. This means you, bull hunter.

The trade volume in industrial supplies is large, at $444 billion, but so is the deficit, at $146 billion. There may be some industries that can help narrow the gap. But we'll have to take a closer look to see.

The total trade in capital goods was the largest, at nearly $500 billion in the first nine months of 2004. The deficit there was also small, both as a number and as a percentage of the total deficit by category. It's here we'll want to look for how a weaker dollar might shift the balance of trade.

Fortunately for data wonks, the BEA does you something of a favor. It breaks down the goods deficit by selected industries. Thus, it's possible to see in which particular industries the United States may be running a goods trade surplus and which industries may be running a goods trade deficit. And by looking at the size of the particular deficit or surplus, we get a picture of where, specifically, a weaker dollar will deliver the most relief (if any). In other words, we can see where to hunt for an investment advantage.

Two tables summarize these categories. Table 8.9 shows most (but not all) of the industries where U.S. firms ran up a goods trade surplus in the first nine months of 2004. Also included is the total dollar volume of trade. This gives you an idea of how much is at stake in the industry if and when dollar weakness leads to more exports. Of course, there's no guarantee that a weak dollar won't cause a general global slowdown and put the kibosh on *all* global trade. But we'll leave the objection aside, for the moment.

What can we conclude from this data deluge, which shows the goods industries that enjoyed a surplus in 2004?

TABLE 8.9   THE SURPRISING TRADE SURPLUSES

Industry	Exports Minus Imports (Billions)	Surplus (Billions)	Total Trade Volume (Billions)
Airplane parts	$11.1–$3.5	+$7.56	$14.7
Airplanes	$18.6–$8.12	+$10.52	$26.7
Animal feed	$2.7–$615 (million)	+$2.13	$3.36
Chemicals—cosmetics	$5.48–$5.03	+$453 (m)	$10.51
Chemicals—dyeing	$3.41–$2.00	+$1.41	$5.42
Chemicals—fertilizer	$1.99–$1.70	+296 (m)	$3.70
Chemicals—n.e.s.	$10.8–$6.0	+$4.7	$16.93
Chemicals—plastics	$18.3–$10.5	+7.8	$28.89
Coal	$2.0–$1.8	+$267 (m)	$3.89
Corn	$4.69–$118 (m)	+$4.5	$4.8
Cotton	$3.54–$16 (m)	+$3.5	$3.56
Hides and skins	$1.2–$60 (m)	+$1.1	$1.26
Metal ores, scrap	$5.6–$3.2	+$2.37	$8.91
Printed materials	$3.6–$3.3	+$288 (m)	$6.91
Pulp and waste paper	$3.3–$2.2	+$1.1	$5.57
Scientific instruments	$24.5–$20.8	+$3.68	$45.41
Specialized industrial machinery	$21.2–$19.4	+$1.84	$40.68

Source: U.S. Department of Commerce, Bureau of Economic Analysis

- *Aerospace is where it's at.* It's a $40 billion market that we already dominate. The European consortium is our main competitor. Boeing is our main exporter.

- *Good chemistry.* Chemicals and plastics have been good to America. Anything that requires more sophisticated chemical treatment can still be done better over here, or at least in terms of volume. The industries that already enjoy a surplus have $62 billion in total trade volumes. And there's more out there.

- *The three Cs.* Corn, cotton, and coal show a combined surplus of $12.2 billion—not huge in real terms. But for resource and commodity investors, it's a good tip that there may be more bullish times ahead for these particular industries.

- *Hides and skins.* The mind boggles at what's included in this category. Are exports of leather and Naugahyde trouncing imports of pachyderm feet and monkey pelts? Alas, there was only $1.2 billion in trade, although there may be a significant black market not reflected in the numbers.

- *Metal ores and scrap.* These data reaffirm the theory that a good business is to buy autos at zero percent down, start a chop shop, and ship the raw materials back overseas at a profit. The parts truly are worth more than the whole! Such is the global economy: destructive creation.

- *Scientific instruments and specialized machinery.* $85 billion between the two. Find the right firm, and you may have a very good business on your hands.

You can see there are some industries where goods trade shows a surplus. How secure or durable that surplus is in an increasingly competitive world is another question. But it's one you look at on a company-by-company basis. You decide which firms are best suited to compete in the twenty-first century on an individual basis. The numbers shown here simply point the bull hunter in the right direction.

But there are other industries, and presumably companies within those industries, that may benefit from a weaker dollar. Some whole industries run a trade deficit, while the dollar volume in trade alone could merit a closer look. And in some cases, the deficit is narrow enough that a large decline in the dollar may indeed tip the balance from deficit into surplus.

Keep in mind, we're only looking at the goods side of the picture. In areas such as music, movies, financial services, and legal services there will be even more opportunity for U.S. firms overseas. Yes, the weaker dollar will hurt. But what you're looking for in the trade numbers are signs that a particular industry is already competitive and may become more so with currency weakness.

There's the possibility that a weaker dollar may *hurt* some companies. But again, that has to be studied on a case-by-case basis. For now, let's look at where the big deficits came from in the first nine months of 2004, and just how big they were, as shown in Table 8.10.

These goods data provide you with three important investment gems:

1. *Lost causes.* Forget about textiles and televisions. American industry is not going to see a revival in making low-cost,

TABLE 8.10   WHERE THE DEFICITS ARE COMING FROM

Industry	Exports	Imports	Deficit (Billions)	Total Trade Volume (Billions)
ADP equipment, office machines	$20.60	$68.02	$47.42	$88
Chemicals—inorganic	$4.46	$5.70	$1.32	$10.2
Chemicals—medicinal	$17.25	$26.08	$8.55	$43.3
Chemicals—organic	$18.24	$26.97	$8.73	$45.2
Electrical machinery	$55.03	$69.09	$14.06	$124.0
Fish and preparations	$2.68	$7.89	$5.21	$10.5
Furniture and bedding	$3.01	$20.41	$17.40	$23.4
General industrial machinery	$25.76	$34.04	$8.27	$59.8
Iron and steel mill products	$5.74	$15.45	$9.71	$21.2
Metal manufacturers, n.e.s.	$8.98	$16.08	$7.09	$25.0
Paper and paperboard	$7.86	$12.20	$4.34	$20.0
Petroleum preparation	$6.77	$26.81	$20.04	$33.5
Power-generating machinery	$26.27	$26.46	$190 (m)	$52.7
Television, VCR	$14.55	$61.62	$47.0	$76.1
Textile, yarn, and fabric	$8.63	$14.62	$5.98	$23.2
Toys, games, sports goods	$2.50	$15.24	$12.73	$17.8
Fruits and vegetables	$6.23	$9.42	$3.18	$15.4
Plastic articles, n.e.s.	$5.53	$8.82	$3.28	$14.3

Source: U.S. Department of Commerce, Bureau of Economic Analysis

finished consumer goods. These deficits are going to get larger, not smaller, over time.

2. *More chemicals.* There is $110 billion more in chemical goods trade up for grabs. The deficits there are small. And the reward for competing more successfully is substantial.

3. *Three big fish.* Electrical machinery, general machinery, and power-generating machinery show trade flows in excess of $60 billion. These are big industries. And with the rest of the world industrializing, it's an intriguing opportunity.

BITING INTO THE EARTH

All economic growth can trace its roots back to tearing up the earth in search of something to eat, burn, or build with. Whether it's stones from a quarry, oil from a well, or wheat from the soil in Kansas, the process of adding value to raw materials means extracting them from the earth in the first place. It takes a little friction to make it all happen.

No matter how you put it, investing in friction isn't sexy. What it really means is investing in capital goods in general, and in construction and agriculture machinery specifically. We're looking for companies that make machines that make machines, or machines that make tools that are indispensable in the kind of heavy industrial activity under way all over the developing world.

In the search for a worthy firm, we're looking first for a good business, next for a bright future, and last for a good price. A lot to ask? Maybe. The entire capital goods industry is surprisingly small, in terms of market capitalization. The entire industry includes 27 firms with a total market cap of about $70 billion. Almost 70 percent of that is made up of just two heavyweights, John Deere (DE, $17 billion) and Caterpillar (CAT, $31 billion).

Both CAT and DE have had nice run-ups since dollar weakness started to make its way to corporate bottom lines in November of 2004. One way to benefit from dollar weakness is to buy a big-cap industrial giant like DuPont (DD), a stock I recommended to my readers in late 2004. What you're looking for is a smaller firm, more leveraged to a falling dollar, and with more of a niche business, rather than the broad diversity of Cat or Deere. We've found one, by way of cemented carbide.

NATURE'S ABRASIVE

If you want to cut metal with metal or drill into rock and stone, you'll want to start with tungsten. In doing my research on tungsten—the key element in the tools made by the firm I'm going to recommend—I wrote a note to Byron King, one of the editors of *Whiskey and Gunpowder,* (whiskeyandgunpowder.com), an e-letter I contribute to. Byron is a geologist. I figured if I wanted a straight answer on why tungsten is critical to the capital goods sector, Byron could give me one.

I asked Byron, "If someone asked you about cemented tungsten carbide and/or rock bits and how nature had selected tungsten to win most battles with abrasion, corrosion, or impact . . . would you think they were daft?" He replied:

It is a perfectly valid observation that instantly catapults you into questions of high order crystallography and physical chemistry. From the standpoint of materials science, tungsten carbide has a hexagonal crystal structure and is almost as hard as diamond. Its melting and boiling points are among the highest of any earthly substance, and it is quite dense considering the atomic weight of what you are working with (i.e., you are packing more substance into a relatively smaller space). Whenever you find something with hexagonal crystal structure, you are looking at a substance with exceptional hardness. In any contest of grinding or abrasion, this structure beats the other crystal structures in nature.

Cemented tungsten carbide is a material that incorporates tungsten carbide into a metal matrix via a sintering process. It is an industrial process of creating a cutting or grinding tool that can continuously place tungsten carbide (almost as hard as diamond) against whatever it is you are trying to cut or shape.

Andrew Mellon and his eponymous bank was an early investor in a formerly Pittsburgh-based company called Carborundum. This was an early abrasives company that pioneered many developments in cutting and grinding tools and machinery. Interestingly, Carborundum's business was also an economic forecaster that was useful to the bank's other interests. When demand for abrasives was rising, it was an early indicator that capital spending was increasing and that the business climate was improving. When demand for abrasives fell, it was the early sign of an impending slowdown. There is still an element of truth to this, although the U.S. economy has been so doped-up on fiat currency and low-interest credit that there is no real telling anymore what the future holds.

Byron is right about not knowing what the future holds. But you can be certain of this: Regardless of what happens in the American economy, earth will be tilled, mines will be dug, wells will be drilled, and tools to shape and cut metal will be needed. The rest of the world, especially China and India, are rapidly catching up on industrialization. That means they are buying and using tangible capital goods at a faster pace than ever. And that means demand for tungsten is growing.

According to the U.S. Geological Survey, more than one-half of the tungsten consumed in the United States was used in cemented carbide parts and wear-resistant materials. Specifically, it was consumed in metalworking, mining, oil and gas drilling, and general construction. There are other applications for tungsten—for example, in filaments for long-lasting lightbulbs and, combined with copper, as a heat sink for electronic goods that generate lots of heat that needs to be dissipated. Because of its physical properties, tungsten works nicely.

But its main industrial application is increasing the hardness and wear resistance of drill bits and metal-cutting tools. When cemented carbide is coated by alumina or titanium nitride it improves the lifetime of the cutting tools by 5 to 10 times. The International Tungsten Industry Association says, "There has been a rapid development in mining and stone cutting tools, with improved performance which has led to the increasing substitution of steel tools by cemented carbide tools, in particular in the oil industry. Notably, the use of very coarse hard metals is growing in this application area."[2]

TURNING TUNGSTEN INTO CEMENTED CARBIDE PRODUCTS

Most of the world's raw tungsten comes from China, Canada, and the former Soviet Union. China, in fact, produces 47 percent of the world's tungsten and is a major exporter as well as consumer. But what the Chinese do not do—yet—is make high-quality cemented carbide tools for use in heavy industry.

That honor is reserved for a handful of American firms. And not by accident. It has taken decades to refine the art of producing hard metals and cemented carbide tools. It is not the sort of operation one gets into easily. There are years of accumulated intellectual capital locked up in the processes and procedures for producing these kinds of capital goods.

That's not to say nature has secrets that can't be discovered by Chinese engineers. But it is the kind of business that's hard to imitate. Either a high-performance drill bit works or it doesn't. Lower-cost substitutes are not preferable if they don't work as well. An American firm, with a weaker dollar, real tangible assets on the balance sheet, and a solid position selling metal-cutting and drilling tools all over the globe is exactly the kind of investment that will thrive in a market where the focus is on real value and not paper assets.

FROM THE LAND OF ROLLING ROCK

Kennametal Inc. (KMT) is one of the country's leading makers of cemented carbide tools. It's the world's second largest provider of metal-cutting tools. And with a global boom in highway construction, oil and gas exploration, and mining, it's going to have an ever larger market in the coming years. It is the quintessential "pick and shovel" stock for the world's second industrial revolution.

The company is based in Latrobe, Pennsylvania. But its four major business segments operate all over the globe, and its sales revenue is globally diversified as well. The two big drivers of revenue growth are the Metalworking Solutions group and the Advanced Materials group.

Total sales for 2004 were $1.9 billion. The metalworking group increased its sales by 10.3 percent to $1.1 billion—more than half the firm's total revenues. The company says, "The business benefited from a market recovery in North America and stronger markets in India, China, and South America."[3]

The Advanced Materials group grew sales at an ever faster rate, 18.6 percent. Kennametal's annual report states, "Mining and construction products were a major contributor to AMSG's performance due to new products and penetration in new markets in 2004. These results were achieved despite continued uncertainty in U.S. highway funding and stagnant markets in Europe and other key global mining economies."[4]

Gross profit is up for the entire firm. Higher sales volume explains part of the $84 million increase. And that's the first leg of what we're looking for—namely, increased demand from around the globe. But the company says "favorable currency effects" also contributed $40.9 million to gross profits.

Two or three more quarters of a weak dollar coupled with growing demand should create even larger gross profits for the firm. And net income is increasing as well. It's the same story with the net as it is with the gross: higher volumes, favorable currency effects, and lower interest expense.

What's even more encouraging is when you see the line-item breakdown of origin of sales. In 2004, the company did about $1 billion in sales to U.S. customers. With a large presence in Germany, it racked up $321 million in Europe's largest economy. It reported $91 million in sales in the United Kingdom and $65 million in Canada.

And then there is "other." The company does not disclose the geographic composition of its "other" revenues, but last year those revenues were $394 million, larger than all of the other major foreign markets it does list. And for all sales, no single customer accounted for more than 10 percent of total sales. Both figures show that KMT has a diverse customer base, both geographically and in terms of numbers. It is not a one-trick pony with only a few large customers.

TANGIBLE ASSETS AND REAL VALUE

As you'd expect for a company of its type, there are more tangible assets than intangible assets on the balance sheet. It lists property, plant, and equipment valued at $484 million. And it's important to note this is the kind of asset (or capital) that keeps on giving. Yes, it wears down and must be depreciated and amortized. But it generates revenue year after year. Long-term debt is $313 million, and the company has more than adequate credit facilities to borrow if it needs to.

How much will this business cost you? KMT is selling for 13 times next year's earnings. It's also selling at less than one times sales. The margins on an industrial economy business are modest, around 4.5 percent last year.

The key will be revenue growth and the market placing a premium on the kind of business KMT is engaged in. On the first score, it will be challenging to expect year-over-year revenue growth of 15 percent in the future. But the weak dollar will deliver a steady currency bonus. And the business itself is being driven by organic growth (which is another way of saying that while the United States chases paper assets, the rest of the world is building factories, digging mines, drilling wells, and laying down roads).

In KMT you find the convergence of a weak dollar and strong overseas demand—not to mention the bull market in energy exploration and mining. Both industries have been undercapitalized for nearly 20 years. As that changes, KMT should benefit.

The risks here are rising raw material costs and a general global slowdown. In either case, the margins get squeezed. But with the metalworking and advanced materials segments generating double-digit revenue growth based on increased demand and new applications for cemented carbides, the future looks . . . shall we say, rock solid.

OTHER PLACES, OTHER BOOKS

If I had the time and space, I would tell you more about the other places I visited in Asia—Thailand in particular, where Debra and Mike Yantis kindly hosted me, took me mountain biking, arranged a ride on a longboat to a nearly deserted island in the Gulf of Siam (except for Buddhist monks), and even had me give a brief presentation to the local Rotary Club. If you are the kind of investor who's ready to make a lifestyle jump, you could do a lot worse than to check out Koh Samui.

In Japan, I felt every bit the foreigner. It helped that my old high school debating partner, Jason Kelly, now lives there. Jason took me up into the mountains and out of the weirdness that is Tokyo. We ate what tasted like barbecued crickets from a Chinese apothecary shop near the waterfalls below Sano. We even went to the hot springs to soak for a while and be gawked at by the locals because of our pale white skin.

China deserves its own book, but I have tried to give you my observations. They are by no means definitive. I hope they're helpful. And if you want to eat the best Peking duck in the world, try Quanjude Roast Duck Restaurant in Beijing.

We have one more stop to make on our bull-hunting tour of the world: the future.

CHAPTER 9

WILDNESS LIES IN WAIT

Capitalism's pre-eminence as a wealth generator means that every tyrant has to either embrace free markets or fall slowly into economic oblivion; but for markets to work, citizens need access to information technology and the freedom to use it—and that means having political power.

—**Robert Wright**[1]

The year is 2050. The Middle Kingdom, formerly known as the People's Republic of China, is the richest, most powerful nation on the planet.

Its thousands of factories hum 24/7, cranking out 60 percent of the world's textiles, sophisticated electronics and computers for the world's IT industry, and over 40 percent of all cars—including the largest auto company in the world, General Motors International, a Chinese blue chip.

A dozen new cities along the eastern coast—sprung up overnight as the result of massive migration from the interior—are packed with skyscrapers that gleam with steel and chrome during the day and glow with neon at night. The Middle Kingdom's middle class, some 300 million strong and young, likes its nightlife.

Massive superhighways and new railroads connect enormous port facilities in Guangzhou, Dalian, and Shenzhen with the rest of the country. Iron ore comes in. Wheat goes out. And oil delivered by pipeline from Russia and from an endless fleet of Saudi tankers ensures the Middle Kingdom will retain its position as the world's number one consumer of oil.

American nannies, yammering in newly learned Mandarin, hustle the children of Beijing's elite merchant class around the Forbidden City, teaching the next generation of entrepreneurs how in less than 100 years a backward and totalitarian nation became the most successful economic story in world history—and did it by design.

But how did they do it?

In retrospect, it should have been easy to see. In the early twenty-first century, the economic problems in America were there for anyone with the wit to see them:

- A $600 billion trade deficit
- A steady loss of high-wage manufacturing jobs to China and Mexico
- A near-zero personal savings rate, high credit card debt, and an epic housing bubble
- A government deficit of some $44 trillion . . . and a series of foreign wars that depleted the country's treasury, polarized the population, and alienated the world

While America spent and gorged and fought costly wars in the Middle East, the People's Republic of China quietly went about building itself an economic dynasty. It made few enemies and many friends—especially in countries rich with the natural resources China so desperately needed.

- *It accumulated more than U.S. $2 trillion and then started spending it* . . . to buy the raw materials and resources it knew it would need in the not-too-distant future.
- *It replaced the United States as the number one destination for foreign direct investment.* China didn't have capital. But it didn't need it. It got the western world to build factories for it.

- *It played a clever strategic game to secure access to the world's most precious commodity: oil.* Without realizing, the United States played exactly into China's hand—alienating the Saudis, who found themselves a new superpower protector in Beijing.

These things happened quietly . . . and, more important, *deliberately.*

Yet few Americans—indeed, few investors at all—were able to grasp what was going on and then take the steps necessary to make windfall profits from it. They missed the opportunity of an investment lifetime.

BACK TO THE PRESENT

It's impossible to predict the future, of course. What I've written is just one way today's events may unfold by 2050. History does not move in straight lines. Human beings make choices. That's one point I hope I've made in the previous chapters. This is an era rich in historical significance. Its events may seem so much larger than life that you can only watch them. You can do more than watch. You can observe, plan, and profit, too.

But it is, admittedly, a complex time in the world's economic history. As an investor, you have tools at your disposal to invest, with precision, in a wide variety of geopolitical and economic trends. Figuring out just what those trends are and which direction they are headed can be daunting.

The bull-hunting method is to combine your personal experience with practical observations from the real world. You can't afford to ignore the world around you anymore, or your investment strategy will be blindsided by events you did not expect and may not understand. However, events are not utterly unpredictable.

OLD MISTRUST, NEW DEPENDENCE

For three days in early June 2004, I spent most of my time waiting at the Indian embassy in Tokyo. I was waiting for a visa to visit India that I hadn't been able to obtain after spending three days at the Indian embassy in Washington, D.C. On each of those three days, I hopped in a cab at my Tokyo hotel and gave the driver a piece of paper with an address on it. The address was written in Japanese characters, but the English name was the Yasukuni Shrine. On each of those three days, each different cab driver paused while looking at the paper and gave me a skeptical look before setting off.

The Japanese are a studiously polite people. You can spend 10 minutes on the subway with your face in someone's back and your armpit in someone else's face, and nobody says a word. I should have known something was up with the shrine, but I didn't think it mattered. I was being dropped off at the shrine only because it was close to the Indian embassy and an easy landmark for cabbies. The Yasukuni Shrine is a symbol for all the troubles Asia faces in its future.

The shrine was erected in 1869 to honor Japanese war dead. Its Japanese name, *Yasukuni Jinja,* means "peaceful nation." Over 2.4 million Japanese are remembered at the shrine. But it's six of them in particular who illustrate the problems Japan and China must overcome in the next century.

After World War II, the International Military Tribunal for the Far East held trials for Japan's 25 wartime leaders. Hideki Tojo and six others were convicted as Class A war criminals and hung till dead. Those six, and Tojo, are honored at the Yasukuni Shrine.

This alone makes the shrine controversial to the victims of Japan's aggression in World War II and its ambitions for a greater Near East. While it is not unusual for victorious nations to honor their war heroes, losing nations are not generally allowed to have heroes, nor to honor them with shrines. It gets even more complicated when the leaders of modern Japan pay regular visits to the shrine to honor the war dead.

The Chinese have taken particular offense to the visits to Yasukuni by current Japanese prime minister Junichiro Koizumi. Koizumi maintains he is honoring the ancestors who made modern Japan possible and that the shrine predates World War II. The Chinese note that the shrine's literature ignores Japan's famous rape of Nanking and that the visits are a way of subtly asserting Japan's independence from China's growing sphere of influence, to borrow a phrase from the Cold War.

Japan and China have a simmering argument left over from World War II. But it really goes back thousands of years. In its current incarnation, it's an argument over who will be important to Asia's future. All the signs point to China's emergence. But both countries have a lot at stake. For years, the United States has been Japan's largest bilateral trading partner. But in 2004, Japan–China trade crossed over the $213 billion mark, accounting for 20 percent of Japanese trade. U.S.-Japanese trade was $197 billion in 2004, or 19 percent of Japanese trade. See Table 9.1.

TABLE 9.1   TOTAL TRADE (GOODS)

Rank	Country	Exports (Year-to-Date)	Imports (Year-to-Date)	Total, All Trade	Percent of Total Trade
—	Total, all countries	745.9	1,342.2	2,088.1	100.0%
—	Total, top 15 countries	559.7	1,011.9	1,571.6	75.3%
1	Canada	172.8	235.1	407.9	19.5%
2	Mexico	101.6	143.2	244.8	11.7%
3	China	31.5	179.2	210.6	10.1%
4	Japan	49.9	118.3	168.2	8.1%
5	Federal Republic of Germany	28.6	70.2	98.9	4.7%
6	United Kingdom	32.9	42.1	75.0	3.6%
7	Korea, South	23.9	42.4	66.3	3.2%
8	Taiwan	19.4	31.7	51.1	2.4%
9	France	19.3	28.7	48.0	2.3%
10	Malaysia	9.9	25.7	35.5	1.7%
11	Italy	9.7	25.4	35.2	1.7%
12	Netherlands	21.9	11.5	33.4	1.6%
13	Ireland	7.3	25.2	32.6	1.6%
14	Singapore	18.2	14.1	32.3	1.5%
15	Brazil	12.7	19.1	31.8	1.5%

Source: U.S. Department of Commerce

The Chinese passed Japan as the United States's third largest trading partner in 2004, as well. China and Japan are now more important to each other, respectively, than the United States is to either. They are bound together by a common geographic bond. They share many of the same markets. Japan has the capital and capital goods that China needs. China has the growing market to sell into that Japanese firms lack domestically. Perhaps most important of all, they both need oil. Then again, so does the rest of the world. But there's only so much oil to go around. Who has it? And who's going to get it? See Figures 9.1, 9.2, and 9.3.

These three figures reveal some stark energy realities. Consumption of oil and natural gas by the developing nations of Asia is going to rise dramatically in the next 20 years. We're seeing the beginning today. It's already driven oil futures into record territory.

Yet the world's oil and gas reserves are located in some of the

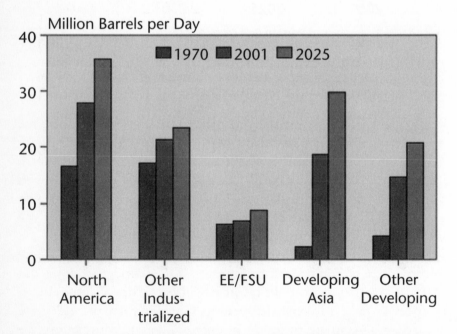

FIGURE 9.1 World Oil Consumption by Region, 1970, 2001, and 2025
(Sources: 1970 and 2001: Energy Information Administration [EIA], *International Energy Annual 2001*, DOE/EIA-0219 [2001], Washington, D.C., February 2003, web site www.eia.doe.gov/iea/. 2025: EIA, System for the Analysis of Global Energy Markets [2003].)

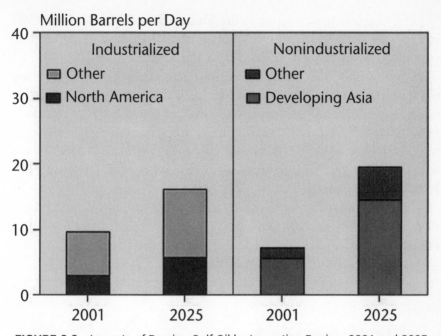

FIGURE 9.2 Imports of Persian Gulf Oil by Importing Region, 2001 and 2025
(Sources: 2001: Energy Information Administration [EIA], *International Energy Annual 2001*, DOE/EIA-0219 [2001], Washington, D.C., February 2003, web site www.eia.doe.gov/iea/. 2025: EIA, Office of Integrated Analysis and Forecasting, IEO2003 WORLD Model run IEO2003.B25 [2003].)

world's most politically volatile and dangerous areas—areas where the United States is not particularly popular today. I'm talking about Venezuela, Saudi Arabia, Russia, and Iran, to name a few. Japan, which imports over 90 percent of its oil, faces a tough choice. Will it side with the United States in the War on Terror and jeopardize its access to energy and friendly relations with the nations that produce it? Or will it take a different path?

The immediate path before Japan is the path of "realism," where energy interests trump idealistic interests. If the world goes down this path, the world's petro-political map will be redrawn along energy alliances. In fact, it's already happening. China in particular has made a flurry of agreements to secure its energy interests with nations the United States considers front lines in the War on Terror.

In this petro-political world, the Saudis, the Iranians, the Chinese, the Russians, and perhaps the Japanese decide that good business

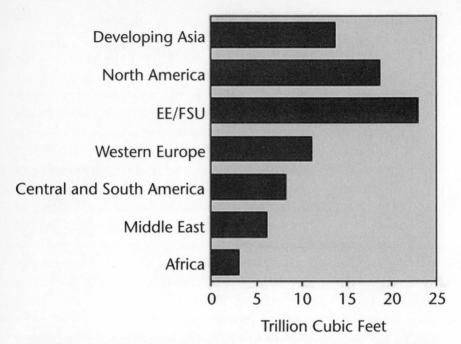

FIGURE 9.3 Increases in Natural Gas Consumption by Region, 2001–2025
(Sources: History: Energy Information Administration [EIA], *International Energy Annual 2001*,
DOE/EIA-0219 [2001], Washington, D.C., February 2003, web site www.eia.doe.gov/iea/.
Projections: EIA, System for the Analysis of Global Energy Markets [2003].)

relations are more important than abstract and intrusive political ideals. The development of the world's economic markets is driven by the self-interest of nations that may have very different political systems but recognize that trading with each other is essential. They stay out of one another's internal affairs and enjoy the fruits of cheap gasoline and steady trade.

ONE *TAMBON,* ONE PRODUCT

As I said, it's nearly impossible to predict how capitalism is going to develop all over the world—especially if it's driven by the geopolitical contest for oil. But the roots of capitalism run deeper than flashy neon signs, four-lane highways, or factories belching black smoke and churning out goods 24/7. In places where capitalism is new, so is the understanding of how free markets work best.

For example, my friends in Thailand, Mike and Debra, tell me that back when the baht crashed in 1997, the government rolled out the "one *tambon,* one product" policy. In order to "get the economy back on its feet," the government told each village (*tambon*) that it could produce only one item. Call it the reverse division of labor, or the concentration of production.

The result, Debra and Mike said, is bizarre. You have whole villages in which everyone produces exactly the same thing and sells it for exactly the same price. The idea, I suppose, is that no one is going to put anyone else out of business and every village will have a monopoly of sorts that supports the economic livelihood of its residents.

The problem, of course, is that you can't command production efficiently, nor can you strip out the role of price in allocating resources and labor effectively to satisfy people's needs and wants. Think about it. One village produces nothing but, hypothetically, canned SPAM. Just SPAM in a can. Maybe people buy it. Maybe they don't. But the village cranks it out no matter what. What if the village can't make enough? What if it makes too much? How does it adjust?

Or take an expensive item like, say, caviar—a whole village cranking out caviar, all at the same price, and regardless of demand. You can see that it simply can't work. Prices communicate valuable information. They tell producers what people want and what they're willing to pay for it. High prices attract more producers because the profit margins are attractive. This brings down prices. As price goes down, demand increases. It's a simple lesson in supply-and-demand curves.

The problem with supply-and-demand curves is that they're static. They take a picture of the marketplace at any given moment. But the market moves. And the only way you can know which way it's moving—how consumers' tastes are changing, what they're willing to pay—is if you allow prices to perform their communicating function.

Laws work in a similar fashion. In order for laws to work best, they have to be easily understandable, transparent, and relatively unchanging, especially in business. If you can't count on conditions remaining relatively predictable in the future, it's difficult to plan.

When the law changes frequently, at the capriciousness of the government, and favors some interest or group over others, it completely breaks down as an effective tool for ensuring the protection of everyone's rights. For this reason, the Austrian economist Friedrich Hayek regarded legislation as the "chief instrument of oppression." You can take your pick of unpopular legislation designed to solve specific problems rather than provide general rules to see how right he is.

Hayek, and the rule of law, are apparently not ideas well received, or even known, to Thailand's stock market regulators. To be fair, it's not just Thailand. It's China, India, Russia, and much of the developing world. One of the future's great questions is how much capitalism in Asia will look like capitalism in the West.

THREE HUNDRED YEARS OF TRIAL AND ERROR

If the West has one thing going for it, it's experience. It takes generations to build up the institutions that make capitalism work—the banks, stock exchanges, bond markets, and insurance companies that get money from those who have it to those who want to put it to work in new ways.

It took 300 years for England to move from a feudal economy dominated by a landed gentry to an industrial economy with sound money and a culture of risk taking and wealth creation. In the end, it was hard to get rich without first being free from the power of the Crown. It was hard to stay rich without having legal rights. It was hard to pass your wealth on to your children without having a culture that valued savings and investment. It was hard for your children to increase that wealth without trade and constant innovation.

The characteristics of Industrial Revolution–era England have become the DNA of a modern, successful, free-market economy. In this economy, freedom is not just an abstract idea. It's a precondition for creating wealth. Can the East get rich without being similarly free? Can China and India jump to the end of the historical learning curve? Will they be able to enjoy all the fruits of a market-based economy without having to develop any of the institutions on which such an economy runs?

We'll see. And don't get me wrong. China and India have plenty of traditions and institutions of their own that have been around far longer than anything in the West. What I wonder is how compatible those traditions and institutions are with what you and I know as capitalism.

But that is a story for another book. What's clear today, regardless of capitalism's future, is that there is plenty of opportunity. Finding your way through the danger is the task of the bull hunter. Happy hunting. Until next time . . .

NOTES

INTRODUCTION

1. Dr. Kurt Richebächer, *The Richebächer Letter,* Agora Financial Publishing, November 2004.
2. James Dyson, Richard Dimbelby Lecture, BBC-1, December 8, 2004, http://news.bbc.co.uk/1/hi/business/4081937.stm.
3. J.R.R. Tolkien, *The Hobbit* (New York: Del Rey Books, 2001).
4. Dyson, Dimbelby Lecture.
5. Ibid.
6. Richebächer, *Richebächer Letter.*
7. Ibid.
8. Dan Blatt, under "Great Acceleration Towards the End," www .futurecasts.com/Depression-descent-end-'31.html.

CHAPTER 1

1. Joseph Schumpeter, *Business Cycles,* (1939; repr. Porcupine Press, 1989).

2. Sir John Templeton, CNBC interview, October 2001, www
   .amazon.com/exec/obidos/tg/detail/-/0971551405/102-5896798-
   6439321?v=glance.
3. Dr. Marc Faber, *The Gloom, Boom, Doom Report,* June 2004.
4. Ed Gramlich, "Subprime Mortgage Lending: Benefits, Costs,
   and Challenges," remarks at Financial Services Roundtable Annual Housing Policy meeting, Chicago, May 21, 2004, www
   .federalreserve.gov/boarddocs/speeches/2004/20040521/default
   .htm.
5. Ibid.
6. Frank Nothaft, *CBSmarketwatch,* www.knowledgeplex.org/news/
   42121.html.

CHAPTER 2

1. Andrew Carnegie, in *The Columbia World of Quotations,* ed.
   Robert Andrews, Mary Biggs, and Michael Seidell (New York:
   Columbia University Press, 1996).
2. Doug Casey, New Orleans Investment Conference, New Orleans,
   November 2, 2004, author's notes.
3. Jim Rogers, New Orleans Investment Conference, New Orleans,
   November 2, 2004, author's notes.
4. John F. Kennedy, from a speech delivered in Indianapolis, In-
   diana, April 12, 1959.

CHAPTER 3

1. Robert A. Heinlein, *Time Enough for Love* (New York: Putnam,
   1973).
2. Ken Fisher, *Money Week* Roundtable, London, September
   2004, www.moneyweek.com/article/407/investing/economics/
   moneyweeks-roundtable.html.
3. American Stock Exchange, www.amex.com, October 7, 2004.
4. China 25 Index iShares (FXI) Fact Sheet, www.ishares.com/
   material_download.jhtml?relativePath=/repository/material/
   downloads/fact_sheet/fxi.pdf.

CHAPTER 4

1. *New York Sun,* August 18, 2004.
2. Howard Davidowitz, CNN/Money, http://money.cnn.com/2004/12/28/news/economy/holidaycreditspending/.

CHAPTER 5

1. Dan Denning, http://eastprofits.blogspot.com/2004/06/bureaucrats-54-dan-two-my-first-full.html.
2. *China Post.*
3. Dan Ferris, *Extreme Value,* September 2004, Stansberry and Associates.
4. Ibid.
5. Anton Chekhov, letter, cited at www.catholicworker.org/dorothyday/datext.cfm?TextID=515.
6. *Plunkett's Energy Industry Almanac* (Houston, TX: Plunkett Research, Ltd., 2005).
7. Ibid.
8. Ibid.
9. Ibid.

CHAPTER 6

1. U.S. Central Intelligence Agency, *The World Factbook,* 2004 edition, www.cia.gov/cia/publications/factbook.
2. Nick Eberstadt, "Power and Population in Asia," *Policy Review,* February 2004, www.policyreview.org/feb04/eberstadt.html. This essay is adapted from a study by the author in Strategic Asia, 2003–2004 (National Bureau of Asian Research).
3. Dr. Marc Faber, *Gloom, Boom, Doom Report,* June 2004.

CHAPTER 7

1. Population Reference Bureau, 2004 World Population Data Sheet, August 2004, www.prb.org/template.cfm?section=PRB&

template=/Content/ContentGroups/Datasheets/2004_World_
Population_Data_Sheet.htm%20%20.
2. Ibid.

CHAPTER 8

1. General Vo Nguyen Giap, *People's War People's Army* (Hanoi:
   Foreign Languages Publishing House, 1961).
2. "The Uses and Applications of Tungsten," International Tungsten
   Industry Association, www.itia.org.uk/tungsten/tungsten_app_
   cem.html.
3. Kennametal Inc., annual report, 2003.
4. Ibid.

CHAPTER 9

Robert Wright, *The New York Times,* January 28, 2005.

INDEX

SPECIAL: For Readers of the book

<u>36% discount</u> on Dan's world-class stock advisory service, *The Bull Hunter* investment advisory.
<u>You can get 15 issues for $49.</u>

We normally offer 12 months for $99 – but we're slashing the price and giving away 3 FREE issues – but ONLY to valued readers of *The Bull Hunter* book.

You can't beat it – right now, **Dan's running an average gain of 26.34%!**

You see, *The Bull Hunter* investment advisory is the venue where Dan's analysis hits the ground running. Join *The Bull Hunter* every month as he tracks down today's hottest investment in the nether reaches of the globe…and delivers the sweet, profitable recommendations right to you.

This is an entirely **risk-free** offer: you'll have 60 days to decide if you want to call in and get a full refund for your Bull Hunter investment advisory subscription.

Here are 2 ways you can immediately place your order for *The Bull Hunter* investment advisory:

CALL: 1-866-215-9065
and give them this Bullhunter discount code:
PHTRF600

ONLINE: Visit **www.bullhunter.com/investment**
and place your order.